Ceviche

Dedicated to all the children in Peru
who are supported by the charity
www.amantani.org.uk

MARTIN MORALES

PERUVIAN KITCHEN

WEIDENFELD & NICOLSON

3♣

8♦

"UNA CONVERSACIÓN
SE EMPIEZA
CON UN BUEN PISCO"

Carlos "Chino" Domínguez

ESTA ES TU CASA

AQUÍ
SE
COCINA
CON CARIÑO

109 PALACIO ARZOBISPAL.—LIMA

61098-C

7♥

Vendedoras de anticuchos
Mercado Central - Lima (Perù)

RAW
LIMA

PERU

CORREOS DEL PERÚ

PERUVIAN KITCHEN

Ceviche

CONTENTS

INTRODUCTION

There is a Peruvian saying my great-aunt Carmela taught me: 'aquí se cocina con cariño', which translated means 'here we cook with loving care'. This is the motto at our restaurant Ceviche – it's what Peruvian food is all about. The other side of what we do is sazón *– the quest to achieve a perfect balance of flavours. I have spent a lifetime working on this. Like most Peruvians, I am obsessed with cooking and I love sharing our amazing food.*

GROWING UP WITH THE FOOD OF PERU

I was born in Lima and spent the first 11 years of my life in Peru. My mother came from a remote village in the Andes and my father from Leicester in the middle of England. In many ways these years of my life were wonderful, not least because they set me on the road to developing my two main passions: music and food.

I was raised in a family that always made sure there was plenty of good food to eat. They made it their business to teach me everything they knew about food – my great-aunts Carmela and Otilia in particular (*pictured left*).

They would take me to the market with them, where I would watch animals destined for the pot running amongst tables piled high with rice, maize, potatoes, and a dizzying array of different fruits, vegetables and herbs. I loved helping my great-aunts in the kitchen; cleaning rice, peeling potatoes and mangoes, podding broad beans – I learnt how to make dishes that I still cook for my children today.

I spent as much time as I could on Makaha beach in Lima, learning to surf and trying to tame the waves. I loved the Pacific Ocean and relished eating all the delicious fish and seafood that came from it. My father would take us to stalls in the nearby district of Chorrillos for ceviche. Sitting on the beach with the sun pounding down on me and my mouth alive with the lime and chilli kick of ceviche was as exhilarating as riding the tallest wave. There is no doubting why ceviche has become Peru's national dish. It is found everywhere – at restaurants, street carts, beach huts – and everyone has their own way of making it. My father also took us on fishing trips that always ended with a barbecue on the beach. Now I appreciate what a luxury it was to be able to eat fish that I had literally just pulled from the sea.

Plaza del Barranco.

REMOTE LIVING

We would occasionally make the arduous journey back to my grandparents' home in the mountains. They lived in a remote Andean village called Cachicadán, well known for its healing thermal waters. At least once every few months my grandmother, 'Mamita Naty', would send her sisters in Lima a hamper of food full of fresh and dried potatoes, home-cured hams, cereals, chancaca honey, beautiful white-green eggs with the deepest of yellow yolks, *rosquitas* (ring-shaped savoury biscuits), tamales and sometimes live poultry reared by her and my grandfather – a turkey for Christmas, and a hen or cockerel at other times. Everything was home-grown or reared and then cooked by my aunties.

Getting to the village was a long and tortuous business. It involved an 18-hour bus ride, winding along treacherous cliff-facing dirt roads, but it was always worth the trip, not least because we were treated to some truly delicious Andean specialities. These included numerous varieties of potatoes I had never tried before and haven't seen since, sweet prickly pears, hearty stews and soups much beloved by the locals, such as *shambar*, made from pork, grains and beans. They also included some wonderful meat dishes, made with my grandparents' own reared, free-range animals, including the guinea pigs that lived happily under the stove in their kitchen, which were delicious either roasted or cooked with chillies and spices.

Thanks to my mother's family, and my father's willingness to let me try all the different kinds of street foods on offer in Lima, I was able to experience every type of food: the Andean dishes still much loved by indigenous people, the street foods made popular by the Afro-Peruvians and Criollos and the wok-cooked dishes available in the many *chifas* (Chinese-Peruvian restaurants) throughout Lima and emulated by my aunties. There were the European-influenced dishes that had become truly Peruvian and finally, of course, the ceviches in all their variations, including those influenced by the Japanese. I loved it all. Buying, cooking and eating food was such an important part of my childhood. Those chefs, street sellers, fishermen, relatives and restaurants all play key roles in my memories – they greatly affected my happiness and who I am now. Little did I know that their everlasting influence would send me on a mission to put Peruvian food on the map in Britain.

MOVING ON

My life in Peru came to an abrupt end when I was 11. After turbulent years of dictatorship and terrorism during the 70s and 80s, Lima was becoming increasingly dangerous. My parents' marriage had broken down and after a very difficult year, which saw my father being threatened by guerrillas, it was decided that my sister and I would move to the UK with my father.

It was a very sad day for me when I left Peru. I was initially very homesick. I missed my mother and the rest of my family, my friends, surfing and the sea, the heat, the warmth and vibrancy of Peru and our land. But the move gave us freedom. For the first time in a year we felt able to walk down the street without the constant fear of danger or violence that came from living in Lima at that time. I embraced life in England and all the opportunities it gave me, but I remained very attached to my Peruvian-Andean roots. I made short trips to Peru every year to visit family, each time learning more about food from my aunts, spending as much time as I could in Barranco, a Bohemian, artistic district of Lima, soaking up the music and the atmosphere, and eating everywhere from the smallest hole in the wall to some of the best Peruvian restaurants.

A NEW CHAPTER

I remained obsessed with Peruvian food. My friends tell me that I have been talking about opening a Peruvian restaurant in London for years. It has clearly always been where my passion lies, despite the fact that I am not a trained chef, just a very enthusiastic home cook. I used to cook for friends and family and could see that Peruvian food appealed to a wide variety of people. In the 90s, I noticed that there was a renewed sense of embracing new cuisine in London.

Throughout most of this time there was only one Peruvian restaurant in London, Fina Estampa, which was owned by a lovely husband-and-wife team. They served traditional Peruvian food with ingredients they were able either to source in Britain or bring back from their trips to Peru. There was also Nobu, which, with its series of selected Japanese and Peruvian dishes, had begun to enchant people on both sides of the Atlantic. However, I wanted an inclusive environment buzzing with life that served Peruvian soul food. I needed to see if I could actually make this happen. So one day I finally stopped talking about opening my own restaurant, and decided to do it. With the full backing of my wife Lucy, I started to put the plans together. Two long years later, after many trials and tribulations, the timing was perfect and the doors of Ceviche finally opened.

OUR RESTAURANT

Peruvian cuisine has always had its fans. For example, the famous French chef Escoffier described it as 'one of the best cuisines in the world'. But it's taken a long time for everyone else to catch on. Over 500 years of fusion has taken place for the cuisine to become what it is today. Starting with indigenous flavours and ingredients and then blending with those brought over by migrants from Spain, Italy, Africa, China and Japan, Peruvian food has evolved into one of the most fascinating, diverse, rich and healthy cuisines in the world. And when made with loving care, there is nothing that beats it.

I had a mission and a clear idea of what the restaurant should be: it had to be fuss-free, neither stuffy nor fine dining, but offering exciting cooking with flair and using the best locally sourced ingredients, led by some key ingredients from Peru. Above all, it had to capture the essence of Peru. All this in a beautifully designed setting. Our restaurant needed to have an interesting location, somewhere central and buzzing to reflect the many great restaurants in Lima. So we chose a building in Soho, London, dating back to 1735, with a house on one side that Mozart once lived and worked in and on the other London's best tattoo parlour.

Our dishes are made with care, *sazón* and great attention to presentation. They are not fussy or overly adorned. They speak for themselves and are honest, healthy and vibrant. Our food is soul food. For you, for everyone.

Ceviche gathers all the signature dishes at our restaurant along with adaptations of traditional recipes from my aunts and grandmother, some of my own new Peruvian dish creations and great recipes by chef Gregor Funcke and our team. This is a collection of recipes that our customers love, that I have grown up with or that have been treasured for hundreds of years. If you haven't tried Peruvian food before, you are in for a real treat.

THE MANY FACES OF PERU

Peru is a nation made up of many races from four continents. The indigenous peoples, including those united under the Incas, and the many independent tribes found today deep in the heart of the Andes grew crops in a highly organised way, including the potatoes and quinoa they held to be sacred. Their cuisine was rich in stews and broths. They used potatoes and chillies, learned how to preserve by drying (*chuños*), used aromatic herbs and ate an early form of ceviche, using a fruit called *tumbo*.

The first main influx of migrants came via the Spanish conquistadors during the 16th century. As well as war and disease, they brought citrus fruits, coriander, onions, garlic and ginger as well as pigs, cattle and chickens. They also brought many European dishes. Some of these originated from the Moorish countries of North Africa, others came from Spanish nuns who built convents in haciendas and were skilled at baking and making desserts.

The Spanish brought over slaves from the Congo and Angola to work in cotton and sugar plantations. Even after emancipation, they were mired in poverty and used to making the most of whatever food they could find. It is thanks to their ingenuity that we have delicious ox-heart *anticuchos*, pumpkin doughnuts and a whole host of stews. The Chinese were not much better off. Brought over as indentured workers in the 1850s, they worked in Peru's guano trade as well as the plantations, but eventually flocked to the cities, especially Lima, where they opened their restaurants and sold the stir-fries or *saltados* that now rank amongst Peru's top dishes. Around the same time the Italians started arriving and brought with them pasta, panettone and Parmesan cheese, so it is hardly surprising that there is a whole fusion involving Chinese stir-fry, Italian spaghetti and Peruvian chillies and spices! Finally, at the end of the 19th century, a wave of migration came from Japan, which particularly influenced the coastal cuisine of Peru, offering an alternative way of making ceviche – the *tiradito* – and introducing some distinctly Japanese flavours, such as mirin and soy. They are often referred to as Nikkei dishes.

Despite the turbulence, natural disasters and political instability in Peru, food has always had a unifying influence. There is no melting pot; just one large kitchen for all to cook in and one large table for all to eat at. Rich and poor, Afro-Peruvian and Criollo, indigenous or of European extraction, we respect each other and our cuisines. So please accept this gift to you, from me, an obsessed foodie who wants to share the joys of Peruvian food.

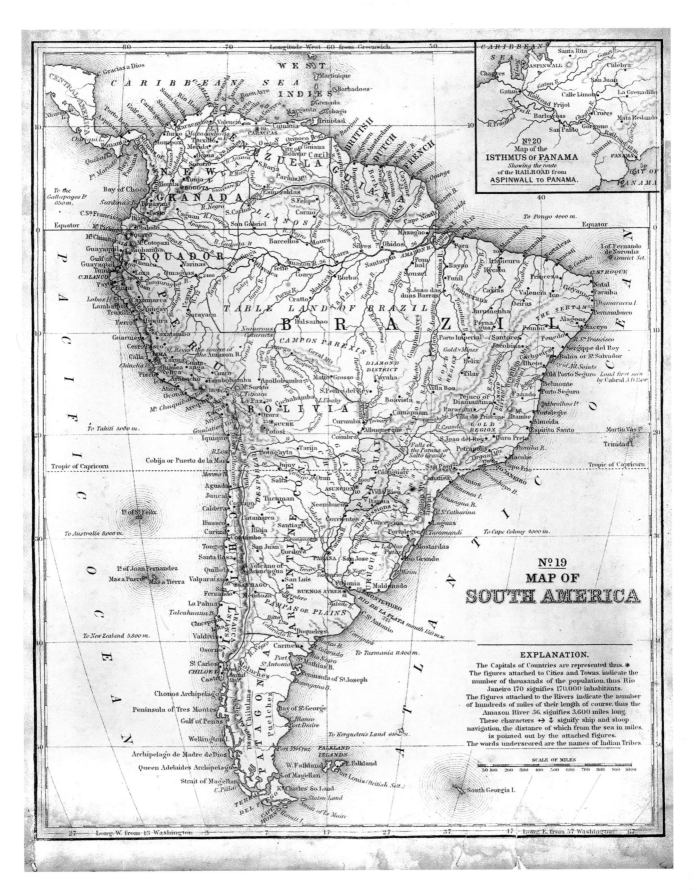

No. 20
Map of the
ISTHMUS of PANAMA
Showing the route
of the RAILROAD from
ASPINWALL to PANAMA.

No 19
MAP OF
SOUTH AMERICA

EXPLANATION.

The Capitals of Countries are represented thus. ✱
The figures attached to Cities and Towns. indicate the
number of thousands of the population. thus Rio
Janeiro 170 signifies 170.000 inhabitants.
The figures attached to the Rivers indicate the number
of hundreds of miles of their length of course. thus the
Amazon River. 36. signifies 3.600 miles long.
These characters ↔ ↨ signify ship and sloop
navigation. the distance of which from the sea in miles.
is pointed out by the attached figures.
The words underscored are the names of Indian Tribes.

SCALE OF MILES
50 100   200   300   400   500   600   700   800   900   1000

1
—
CEVICHES

A FEW THOUSAND YEARS AGO, PEOPLE FROM THE COASTAL REGIONS OF PERU WERE EATING A VARIATION OF TODAY'S CLASSIC CEVICHE. *I imagine that the fishermen who braved the seas knew that they could easily sustain themselves with some fresh catch dressed with Peru's own amarillo chilli and the acidic juice of the indigenous fruit known as* tumbo.

The dish recognised as ceviche today is very similar to that made thousands of years ago. It evolved thanks to ingredients brought to Peru by the Spanish, such as onions and a variety of citrus fruit; particularly the lime. The concept of ceviche is very simple: take the freshest fish or seafood you can get hold of, 'cook' it for a few minutes in a citrus-based marinade (known as 'tiger's milk' or leche de tigre*) and then serve immediately.*

In the late 19th century, the arrival of Japanese migrants brought a unique way of cutting fish, leading to the invention of the tiradito. *It is a type of ceviche, but the difference is in the way the fish is sliced – similar to sashimi or carpaccio. Tiradito rarely contains onions, has a lighter taste and is marinated in a tiger's milk that will sometimes include Eastern flavours, such as soy, mirin and ginger.*

Today ceviche is the national dish of Peru. It is such a celebrated dish that it even has a day to itself – National Ceviche Day. There are endless combinations and recipes and every Peruvian has their own way of making it.

Two things are key to a good ceviche: tiger's milk, which is explained further on page 229, and fresh fish. You should always buy the freshest fish you can and use it as soon as possible for the best taste. The type of fish you use is important, but you can always vary it according to what is available. Fish suitable for ceviche can be divided into three texture categories: firm, medium and soft. Firm fish such as monkfish, hake and cod will have to 'cook' in tiger's milk for twice as long as a medium fish. Sea bass, snapper, sea bream, tilapia, stone bass, rock bass, halibut, sole, tuna and salmon are all medium-textured fish. Mullet, whiting and mackerel are soft textured and will need half the amount of 'cooking' time to a medium-textured fish. At Ceviche, we like to use sea bass as we find it the most delicious and the most readily available, but you could use any firm white fish.

At the restaurant we always source sustainable fish and seafood – naturally, we want to make sure that we can all enjoy eating fish forever more. The recipes all specify filleted amounts of fish. However, it is more economical to buy whole fish, because that way you can use the bones and offcuts to make stock, which is useful for some of the recipes later in the book. If you are unsure about filleting fish yourself, ask your fishmonger to do it for you.

DON CEVICHE

SEA BASS CEVICHE *This is our signature dish, so called as it's really the daddy of all our ceviches and the most popular dish we serve at Ceviche. We suggest sea bass for this recipe, but use whatever is freshest at market – try sea bream, Dover sole or any other firm-textured white fish.*

Wash the sliced red onion and then leave it to soak in iced water for 5 minutes. Drain thoroughly, spread out on kitchen paper or a clean tea towel to remove any excess water and then place in the fridge until needed. This will reduce the strength of the onions and help to keep them crisp.

Cut the fish into uniform strips of around 3 x 2cm. Place in a large bowl, add a good pinch of salt and mix together gently with a metal spoon. The salt will help open the fish's pores. Leave this for 2 minutes and then pour over the tiger's milk and combine gently with the spoon. Leave the fish to 'cook' in this marinade for 2 minutes.

Add the onions, coriander, chilli and the cubed sweet potato to the fish. Mix together gently with the spoon and taste to check the balance of salt, sour and chilli is to your liking. Divide between serving bowls and serve immediately.

NOTES

♦ Keep your fish refrigerated until just before using.

♦ We recommend using fine sea salt for making any kind of ceviche as it is higher quality than other salts and more beneficial in cold 'cooking'. With any other kind of cooking with heat normal table or rock salt is sufficient.

SERVES 4

1 large red onion, very thinly sliced

600g sea bass fillet (or other white fish), skinned and trimmed

1 portion of Amarillo Chilli Tiger's Milk (see page 230)

A few coriander sprigs, leaves finely chopped

1 limo chilli, deseeded and finely chopped

1 sweet potato, cooked and cut into small cubes (see page 221)

Fine sea salt

CONCHAS BORRACHAS

DRUNK SCALLOPS *I have always been a huge fan of scallop sashimi. After experimenting with various flavour combinations and some trial and error, this scallop dish was born. It's one of the prettiest, most delicate and most loved dishes on our menu.*

SERVES 4

12 large scallops, each cut
   into 3 thin slices
2 limes, cut in half
Seeds from ½ a pomegranate
1 limo chilli, deseeded and finely chopped
2 tbsp pisco (or a good-quality vodka)
4 tbsp Coriander Oil (see page 235)
A small handful of freshly torn coriander
   leaves or micro coriander
Fine sea salt

Arrange the slices of scallop on serving plates. Don't worry if you have to overlap them slightly. Sprinkle some salt over them and squeeze half a lime over each plate.

Sprinkle with the pomegranate seeds and chilli and then drizzle over a few drops of pisco or vodka and the Coriander Oil. Decorate with coriander or micro coriander leaves and serve straight away.

NOTE

♦ Rather than serving straight on a plate you could also serve these scallops on clean scallop shells.

ALIANZA LIMA

MIXED SEAFOOD & FISH CEVICHE *All Peruvians love football. The Alianza Lima football team brings together a mix of players, enriching the way they play. These characteristics have inspired this colourful ceviche, which combines different varieties of seafood and fish.*

SERVES 4

1 large red onion, very thinly sliced

160g sea bass fillet (or other white fish), skinned and trimmed

12 large raw tiger prawns, peeled, deveined and blanched in salted boiling water for 1 minute

100g octopus, cooked and cut into 3cm cubes

1 portion of Rocoto Tiger's Milk (see page 230)

50g cooked choclo (see page 223) or sweetcorn kernels

10g coriander leaves, finely chopped

100g sweet potato, cooked and cut into small cubes (see page 221)

1 limo chilli, deseeded and finely chopped, plus extra sliced chilli to garnish

Fine sea salt

Wash the sliced red onion and then leave to soak in iced water for 10 minutes. Drain thoroughly, spread out on kitchen paper or a clean tea towel to remove any excess water and then place in the fridge until needed.

Cut the fish into uniform strips of around 3 x 2cm, put in a bowl and sprinkle with a good pinch of salt. After 2 minutes, add the prawns, octopus and tiger's milk. Leave to 'cook' for 2 minutes. Add the cooked choclo or corn kernels, strained onions, coriander, sweet potato and chopped chilli and mix gently with a spoon.

Serve immediately, garnished with finely sliced limo chilli and extra coriander leaves if desired.

CEVICHE TRAVELS

Ceviche comes in all shapes and sizes throughout Latin America. In some countries they like to add tomatoes, red peppers and even ketchup, others leave their ceviches 'cooking' in citrus juices for hours on end, taking the subtlety of the freshness away from the dish. In Peru and at Ceviche, we think simplicity is best, and so, as every great *cevichero* will tell you, all you need is fresh fish, tasty Peruvian chillies, lime juice and salt.

SAKURA MARU

SALMON TIRADITO Sakura Maru *was the name of the ship that brought the first Japanese immigrants to Peru. This Nikkei-inspired dish is a nod to their rich culture and that important moment when they arrived on Peruvian shores.*

SERVES 4

Vegetable oil, for frying

A small handful of rice vermicelli
   (be careful not to break them)

2 spring onions

½ red onion, finely chopped

1 large tomato, deseeded
   and finely chopped

2 tbsp finely chopped coriander leaves

400g salmon fillets, skinned and trimmed

1 portion of Nikkei Tiger's Milk
   (see page 230)

Fine sea salt

Prepare the garnishes. Half fill a saucepan with vegetable oil and heat until smoking. Add the vermicelli and cook for just 10 seconds. The noodles will immediately start to puff up and turn opaque. Remove immediately and drain on kitchen paper. Cut the spring onion whites and half the greens on the diagonal, about 2mm thick. Mix the red onion, tomato and coriander together in a bowl.

Cut the fish as finely as you can diagonally across the grain into very thin slices – you should end up with slices that look very similar to shop-bought smoked salmon.

Arrange the salmon slices on plates. Pour some tiger's milk on each of them and add a little salt to flavour if needed. Add some onion and tomato mix on top of the salmon and arrange the spring onions around it. Finish each plate by putting some of the puffed vermicelli on top of the onions to give the dish some height and crunchiness.

NOTE
♦ You can make a larger batch of the fried vermicelli if you like as they keep very well in an airtight container.

NIKKEI: THE JAPANESE–PERUVIAN CULTURE

Just over 100 years ago the first Japanese migrants set sail for Peru on the *Sakura Maru*, hoping for a better life. Peru is now home to the fifth largest Japanese community outside Japan and has managed to absorb the best of Japanese customs and culinary traditions. 'Nikkei' cuisine is rooted in a respect for the foods of both Peru and Japan. They have much in common, not least a reverence for the freshest fish and seafood. The result of this collaboration of culinary forces is a seamless fusion of delicious foods and dishes that have become some of the most loved in Peru.

TIRADITO DE CABALLA

MACKEREL TIRADITO WITH GOOSEBERRY TIGER'S MILK *This* tiradito *combines Peruvian techniques with the best of British ingredients. It's a wonderful recipe to try in the early summer when both gooseberries and mackerel are at their best.*

SERVES 4

4 mackerel fillets, skinned, de-boned
    and trimmed
1 tsp sea salt
Juice of 2 limes
1 small red onion, very thinly sliced
1 tbsp crumbled pecans
1 dried panca chilli, ground
    or finely chopped (see Note)
2 tsp capers

FOR THE GOOSEBERRY TIGER'S MILK
Juice of 2 limes
100g gooseberries
Juice of ½ an orange
1 tbsp Amarillo Chilli Paste (see page 226)
A pinch of fine sea salt

Cut the mackerel fillets in half lengthways and put them in a bowl with the salt and the lime juice. Leave to 'cook' for about 5 minutes.

Put all the tiger's milk ingredients in a food processor or blender and blitz until smooth. Strain the liquid through a sieve to remove any gooseberry seeds.

Cut the marinated mackerel fillets diagonally across the grain so you end up with very thin, wide slices and divide between 4 serving plates (reserving the tiger's milk).

Drizzle over the tiger's milk and then top with the red onion, crumbled pecans, panca chilli and capers. Season with salt before serving.

NOTE
♦ Panca chillies can be ground very easily in a pestle and mortar or a spice or coffee bean grinder, but remember to discard the seeds first.

CEVICHE A LA PARRILLA

HOT POLLOCK & CLAM CEVICHE *This ceviche is a bit special as the fish and clams are charred over a hot grill, giving the whole dish a lovely smoky flavour.*

Put the fish, clams, lime juice, spring onions, amarillo chilli and paste in a bowl and season to taste with fine sea salt. Stir gently to mix.

Prepare your barbecue (a coal one is best for this dish) or a griddle pan and ensure it is hot before cooking.

Open 2 of the corn husks and place them on top of each other. Repeat this 4 times so you create 4 corn husk plates.

Spoon the fish and clam mixture on top of the husk plates, reserving some of the marinade. Carefully place each of the filled husk plates on the prepared barbecue or griddle pan. Cook for 5–7 minutes over a low to medium heat.

Carefully lift the filled husks off the barbecue (avoiding any spillage) and place them on a serving dish. Drizzle with the reserved marinade and sprinkle with coriander before serving.

SERVES 4

4 pollock fillets, cut into 2cm cubes
20 medium-sized clams, washed and dried
Juice of 8 limes
2 spring onions, finely chopped
1 amarillo chilli
2 tbsp Amarillo Chilli Paste (see page 226)
8 large corn-on-the-cob husks,
    washed in cold water
1 large bunch of coriander,
    leaves finely chopped
Fine sea salt

BARRANCO I LOVE YOU

SEA BASS & GREEN MANGO TIRADITO *The Barranco district of Lima is an exciting neighbourhood filled with restaurants and bars that attract musicians, poets, writers and bohemians. Barranco is full of colour and history, and its proximity to the sea and stunning surroundings makes the cooking in its restaurants dynamic, diverse and entertaining. We had its spirit very much in mind when creating our restaurant in London, so we had to name a recipe after it.*

Cut the fish as finely as you can diagonally across the grain into very thin slices. Arrange the fish on 4 plates, add a sprinkle of salt and leave for 2 minutes.

Meanwhile, grate the mango half and add the gratings to a bowl with a squeeze of orange juice.

Pour over the tiger's milk and add the mango. Sprinkle with limo chilli and the chopped or micro basil to finish.

SERVES 4

400g sea bass fillet (or other white fish), skinned and trimmed
½ green mango, peeled
A squeeze of orange juice
½ portion of Amarillo Chilli Tiger's Milk (see page 230)
1 limo chilli, deseeded and very finely chopped
Chopped basil leaves or micro basil
Fine sea salt

ENROLLADO DE QUINUA Y CEVICHE

QUINOA & CEVICHE ROLLS *This elegant way of serving ceviche is reminiscent of sushi in appearance. Instead of using rice, quinoa is used, giving a lovely light and nutty flavour. You don't need much fish and you could use any mild-tasting white fish such as sea bass or whiting.*

SERVES 4

2 tbsp black sesame seeds, dry roasted
200g cooked quinoa, well-drained
2 nori sheets, cut in half horizontally
120g white fish fillets, such as sea bass,
   cut into thick slices
½ portion of Nikkei Tiger's Milk
   (see page 230)
1 ripe avocado, cut into thick batons

TO SERVE
Pickled sushi ginger
Soy sauce
2 tbsp Rocoto Jam (see page 233)

Mix the dry roasted sesame seeds with the well-cooked quinoa in a bowl.

Lay a sheet of cling film on top of a sushi mat. Spread a quarter of the quinoa mixture evenly over the cling film using your hands or a spatula, pressing down lightly as you go and leaving a 1cm border along the top edge. Place a nori sheet on top, shiny side down.

Put a quarter of the fish in a bowl with the tiger's milk and leave for 30 seconds. Remove the fish with a slotted spoon and arrange on top of the nori sheet along with the avocado.

Carefully but firmly roll the mat peeling back the cling film to keep it from being caught and rolled into the centre. Squeeze the roll slightly to make sure it is completely even and that the quinoa doesn't spill. Repeat the process with the remaining nori sheets and filling until you have 4 rolls.

Cut each roll into 6 slices and serve with ginger, soy sauce and some of the Rocoto Jam.

CEVICHE ANTIGUO

ANTIQUE ROCOTO FISH CEVICHE *During the months when Seville oranges are available, try this ceviche, as it is best made with sour oranges. At other times of the year you can make the tiger's milk with equal quantities of freshly squeezed orange juice and lime juice.*

SERVES 4

1 large red onion, very thinly sliced
600g halibut fillet (or other white fish), skinned and trimmed
1 portion of Rocoto Tiger's Milk (see page 230) made with 2 juicy Seville oranges instead of limes and add a pinch of sugar
2 radishes, finely sliced with a vegetable peeler
A few coriander leaves
1 amarillo chilli, deseeded and finely sliced
Fine sea salt

Wash the sliced red onion and then leave to soak in iced water for 10 minutes. Drain thoroughly, spread out on kitchen paper or a clean tea towel to remove any excess water and then place in the fridge until needed.

Cut the fish into uniform strips of around 3 x 2cm and put them in a large bowl. Add some salt and mix together gently with a metal spoon. The salt will help open the fish's pores. Leave this for 2 minutes, pour over the tiger's milk and combine gently with the spoon. If you are using Seville oranges, leave the fish to 'cook' in the marinade for around 1 hour as the sour oranges are not as strong as limes.

Add the onion, radish, coriander and chilli to the fish. Mix together gently, taste to ensure the levels of salt and citrus are well balanced and, once happy, divide between bowls. Serve immediately.

IS IT ALL ABOUT LIMES?

While in Peru we experiment with other fruit such as clementines and grapefruit, lime is the 'king' in ceviches, but this wasn't always the case. In pre-colonial times, before citrus fruits had been brought to Latin America, the traditional and more commonly used fruit was the fresh or fermented juice of the *tumbo* – a kind of elongated passion fruit. When the Spanish conquistadors arrived and discovered the dish, they preferred sour oranges. This antique version, using Seville oranges, is our take on these early ceviches.

CHACALÓN

MUSHROOM & SWEET POTATO CEVICHE *Chacalón was one of my favourite Peruvian chicha music stars. Like chicha music, this vegetarian dish is colourful and humble, and in this recipe we try to capture Chacalón's vibrant spirit.*

Put the mushrooms, olives, cooked sweet potato, spring onions and red onion into a bowl and season with salt and freshly ground black pepper.

Mix the clementine juice and caster sugar with the tiger's milk in a bowl until the sugar has dissolved. Add the vegetables and mix well. Taste to ensure it is well seasoned and the flavours are balanced. Leave for a couple of minutes to marinate and then arrange the vegetables over 4 serving plates, drizzling over any juices from the marinade.

Garnish with the limo chilli and the coriander.

SERVES 4

160g fresh mushrooms, quartered
60g pitted Peruvian botija olives
    (or kalamata or any other black olives)
120g cooked sweet potato,
    cut into small cubes (see page 221)
3 spring onions, finely sliced
1 small red onion, finely diced
2 tbsp clementine juice
½ tbsp caster sugar
1 portion of Rocoto Tiger's Milk
    (see page 230) made without
    the fish cuttings
1 limo chilli, deseeded and finely chopped
A few coriander sprigs, leaves chopped
Fine sea salt and freshly ground
    black pepper

2
—
STREET FOOD

STREET FOOD IN PERU HAS CHANGED A LOT OVER THE YEARS *due to a variety of cultural influences, cooking styles and available ingredients, but one thing has remained consistent: it packs a punch in flavour. In Lima, it's the battle of the carts as street sellers compete heavily for business. There's a bustling, exciting atmosphere. It is impossible to imagine Lima without thinking of those sizzling ox-heart skewer (*anticuchos*) or hot sandwich (*sanguches*) sellers working side-by-side on street corners all around the city, turning out mountains of delicious street food to thousands of satisfied customers.*

It used to be a risky business visiting some of my favourite sellers as a child because the best food was in areas rife with crime. But we used to risk it, watching our backs and diving straight into the car as soon as we had our hands on the food. Fortunately, the streets are now a lot safer.

Some of the best street food comes from Afro-Peruvian culture. Afro-Peruvians were inventive in their use of humble ingredients; what they chose was driven by what they had available, but this only helped to improve the flavour of their dishes. For example, ox heart is used rather than prime steak, being just as tender on a skewer.

I urge you to dive into this varied selection of dishes and experience what I believe is the most exciting street food in the world. Some dishes are classics from the streets of Lima, Cuzco or elsewhere in Peru, and others are recipes that have been inspired by these classics or the techniques used, but reimagined by us.

ANTICUCHOS DE CORAZÓN

OX-HEART SKEWERS *These skewers of marinated meat are so much more than a street food snack to Peruvians; they bring back memories of cold nights outside football stadiums, the air thick with the smoky aroma of cumin, chilli and old coal grills from street sellers' carts.*

First, make the marinade. You will need to prepare this several hours before cooking. Soak the dried panca chilli in warm water for 5–10 minutes if using. Put the soaked chilli (or the fresh chilli and paprika if using instead) in a food processor or blender with the remaining marinade ingredients and blitz together until smooth.

Put the ox heart into a non-reactive bowl and pour over the marinade. Cover and chill for several hours, or overnight if possible. Remove the meat from the fridge and leave it to return to room temperature before cooking.

Thread the meat onto the metal or soaked bamboo skewers, reserving some of the marinade for basting.

Prepare your grill, barbecue or griddle pan. You need to get it really hot. If you are using a griddle pan, heat it for 5 minutes and test to ensure it's very hot before cooking.

Cook the skewers, placing several on the hot barbecue or griddle pan at a time, for 2 minutes. Turn over and cook for another 2 minutes. Keep basting with the reserved marinade until the meat has taken on a rich, caramel sheen. It should still be slightly pink in the centre.

Serve with the Amarillo Chilli Sauce and some Salsa Criolla.

VARIATION
♦ You can substitute ox heart for rump steak or even large, meaty portobello mushrooms if you prefer.

SERVES 4

600g ox heart, trimmed
    and cut into thin strips
1 portion of Amarillo Chilli Sauce
    (see page 232)
1 portion of Salsa Criolla (see page 236)
12–16 metal skewers or bamboo skewers
    soaked in water until ready to use

FOR THE MARINADE
4 tbsp Panca Chilli Paste (see page 226)
2 garlic cloves, crushed
2 tbsp olive oil
125ml red wine vinegar
1 tbsp ground cumin
1 tsp dried oregano
Salt

ANTICUCHOS DE PULPO Y SALCHICHA DE HUACHO

OCTOPUS & HUACHANA SAUSAGE SKEWERS *Peruvian huachana sausage can be very difficult to get hold of, which is why we've included a recipe (see page 238) for you to make it from scratch. But don't worry if making sausages is not your thing; make these with chorizo as an alternative – they taste just as good.*

Place the octopus in a deep saucepan with the garlic, bay leaf and black peppercorns. Cover with a lid and cook over low heat for about 2 hours until tender – don't add any water or salt. Cut the tentacles from the body of the octopus and discard the rest. Cut the tentacles into 3cm long chunks.

Put all the marinade ingredients in a bowl and mix well. Add the cooked octopus and sausage and leave for about 10 minutes to marinate.

Prepare your grill, barbecue or griddle pan. You need to get it really hot. If you are using a griddle pan, heat it for 5 minutes and test to ensure it's very hot before cooking.

Assemble the skewers, alternating the marinated octopus and sausage (and reserving the marinade).

Cook the skewers on the hot grill, barbecue or griddle pan for about 5 minutes, turning regularly and basting with the reserved marinade until they are nicely browned and charred on all sides. Be careful as the sausage will release a lot of fat and spit at you.

Serve with the Amarillo Chilli Sauce and some Salsa Criolla.

SERVES 4

1 large octopus, weighing 1–2kg
1 garlic clove
1 bay leaf
1 tsp black peppercorns
300g chorizo or Huachana Sausages (see page 238), cut into 3cm slices
1 portion of Amarillo Chilli Sauce (see page 232)
1 portion of Salsa Criolla (see page 236)
12–16 metal skewers or bamboo skewers soaked in water until ready to use

FOR THE MARINADE

2 garlic cloves, crushed
1 tsp dried oregano
1 tbsp Amarillo Chilli Paste (see page 226)
50ml olive oil

ANTICUCHOS DE HÍGADO DE POLLO

CHICKEN LIVER SKEWERS *The flavour of chicken liver marries brilliantly with the cumin, chilli and vinegar in the marinade, but cubes of chicken or salmon would work equally well.*

SERVES 4

400g chicken liver, trimmed and cut in half
1 portion of Amarillo Chilli Sauce
  (see page 232)
1 portion of julienned Salsa Criolla
  (see page 236)
12–16 metal skewers or bamboo skewers
  soaked in water until ready to use

FOR THE MARINADE

2 garlic cloves, crushed
4 tbsp Amarillo Chilli Paste (see page 226)
2 tbsp olive oil
125ml red wine vinegar
1 tbsp ground cumin
½ tsp salt
½ tsp freshly ground black pepper

Mix together all the ingredients for the marinade in a bowl and add the chicken liver. Cover and leave to marinate for 1–2 hours.

Prepare your grill, barbecue or griddle pan. You need to get it really hot. If you are using a griddle pan, heat it for 5 minutes and test to ensure it's very hot before cooking.

Thread the marinated chicken liver (reserving the marinade) onto the soaked skewers.

Cook the skewers on the hot grill, barbecue or griddle pan, turning regularly and basting with the reserved marinade for about 5–6 minutes until they are nicely golden and just cooked through.

Serve with the Amarillo Chilli Sauce and some Salsa Criolla.

THE ANTICUCHERAS OF LIMA

Anticuchos are the ultimate leveller as they're available from street carts and up-market restaurants alike. They're the main source of income for the hardworking, entrepreneurial *anticucheras* – the women who set up every night on street corners in Lima. Some of these *anticucheras* have become cult figures thanks to their indomitable spirit and, of course, their delicious barbecued skewers.

CAMARONES Y ESPÁRRAGOS EN QUINUA

QUINOA-COATED PRAWNS & ASPARAGUS *This recipe, by one of our talented chefs, Alejandra Breustedt, uses quinoa to provide a lovely nutty crunch and textured coating that is a tasty alternative to breadcrumbs.*

Put the prawns and asparagus in a bowl. Season with salt and pepper and then pour over the lime juice. Leave to marinate while you make the batter.

Make sure the quinoa is as dry as possible; if necessary, spread it out on a baking tray and put it in a very low oven for a few minutes so any moisture will steam off. When it has cooled down, put it in a bowl. Put the flour in another bowl and season it with salt and pepper. Whisk the eggs with the olive oil in another separate bowl until well blended.

Drain the prawns and asparagus. Coat them in the flour and tap gently to dust off any excess. Dip them in the egg mixture and, finally, give them a generous covering of the quinoa.

If you have a deep-fat fryer, heat the vegetable oil to 180°C. If not, pour the oil to a depth of about 5cm in a large, deep saucepan, making sure that it is no more than half full. To test if the oil is hot enough, drop in a cube of bread; if it sizzles and turns golden, the oil is ready. Fry the prawns and asparagus in batches for a couple of minutes per batch until crisp and golden all over. Drain on kitchen paper and serve immediately with the Rocoto Jam and soy sauce for dipping.

SERVES 4

12 large prawns, peeled and deveined
12 tender asparagus, woody stalks
    removed
Juice of 2 limes
Vegetable oil, for deep-frying
Rocoto Jam (see page 233), for dipping
Soy sauce, for dipping
Salt and freshly ground black pepper

FOR THE BATTER

200g cooked quinoa, drained
100g plain flour
2 large eggs
20ml olive oil

BOLAS DE YUCA

CASSAVA & CHEESE CROQUETTES *Cassava is believed to be one of the oldest tubers grown in Peru. You might recognise it by its other name, yuca. You can buy it fresh from some West Indian or African markets or frozen from Indian shops.*

MAKES 8

250g cassava, peeled, fibrous parts
   discarded and cut into chunks
1 tbsp Amarillo Chilli Paste (see page 226)
3 garlic cloves, crushed
25g butter
1 egg yolk
Juice of 1 lime
50g mature Cheddar cheese
Vegetable oil, for frying
1 portion of Huancaina Sauce
   (see page 232)
Salt and freshly ground black pepper

FOR THE COATING

1 egg, beaten
50g panko breadcrumbs (or fresh
   and dried breadcrumbs)
Flour, for dusting

Bring a saucepan of water to the boil and add some salt. Add the cassava and cook until it is soft – this should take at least 30 minutes. Strain the cassava and mash (using a mouli if possible) immediately while it is very hot. Add the Amarillo Chilli Paste, crushed garlic, butter, egg yolk and lime juice. Season with salt and pepper and mix thoroughly.

When the mixture has cooled down and firmed up a bit, divide it into 8 portions. Cut the cheese into 8 cubes. Use your hands to mould the portions of cassava mixture around each piece of cheese so that the cheese is completely encased by the cassava mixture. Shape into balls roughly the size of golf balls.

Put the beaten egg and the breadcrumbs in separate shallow bowls. Dust the balls in flour and then dip each one into the egg and then in the breadcrumbs.

If you have a deep-fat fryer, heat the vegetable oil to 170°C. If not, pour the oil to a depth of about 5cm in a large, deep saucepan, making sure that it is no more than half full. To test if the oil is hot enough, drop in a cube of bread; if it sizzles and turns golden, the oil is ready.

Fry the balls in the hot oil, turning, until they are golden brown all over. Cook in batches to avoid overcrowding.

Drain the croquettes on kitchen paper and serve while still hot with a side of Huancaina Sauce.

SANGUCHE DE CHICHARRÓN

PORK & SWEET POTATO ROLLS *This favourite Peruvian breakfast is commonly served in separate parts, which you are then left to assemble yourself. More and more cafés and takeaways are bringing these together in a ready-to-eat roll.*

Cut the pork into fairly large chunks and rub all over with the salt. Leave to marinate for at least a few hours, but preferably overnight.

When you are ready to cook the pork, rinse it well to remove the salt and pat dry with kitchen paper. Place the pork in a wide-based saucepan. Scantily cover the pork with water, add the onion and bay leaves and bring to the boil over medium heat. Skim off any foam that appears on the surface and then partially cover. Leave to simmer over low heat until the water has completely evaporated. Test the pork for tenderness by piercing the meat with a fork or skewer. If it is not yet falling apart, add some more water and continue to simmer.

Take the lid off and let the pork fry in its own fat over high heat, turning regularly and adding a little oil if needed, until it is crispy and golden brown and the meat is very tender. This should take about 20–30 minutes.

Cut the sweet potatoes into thin strips, a similar size to French fries. If you have a deep-fat fryer, heat the vegetable oil to 170°C. If not, pour the oil to a depth of about 5cm in a large, deep saucepan, making sure that it is no more than half full. To test if the oil is hot enough, drop in a cube of bread; if it sizzles and turns golden, the oil is ready. Dust the sweet potatoes with potato or rice flour and deep-fry them until they are golden and crisp.

Fill the crusty rolls with the pork, sweet potato fries, plenty of Salsa Criolla and some Amarillo Chilli Sauce if using.

VARIATION

♦ You could also bake the sweet potato fries in an oven preheated to 200°C (gas mark 6). Simply spread the sweet potato batons out on a baking sheet, drizzle with oil and bake for 15–20 minutes until golden and crisp.

SERVES 4

1kg pork shoulder (or pork belly)
2 tbsp salt
1 onion, halved
2 bay leaves
Vegetable oil, for frying (optional)
4 round white crusty bread rolls
  (Ciabatta rolls)
1 portion of julienned Salsa Criolla
  (see page 236)
1 portion of Amarillo Chilli Sauce
  (see page 232), optional

FOR THE SWEET POTATO FRIES

2 sweet potatoes, peeled
Potato or rice flour, for dusting
Vegetable oil, for deep-frying

TEQUEÑOS DE AJÍ DE GALLINA

CHICKEN SPRING ROLLS *A Peruvian take on classic spring rolls, these crispy bites are creamy and moreish. Here is a version based on an absolute classic: a spicy chicken dish we love called* ají de gallina. *You can fill them with anything that takes your fancy, though – try a combination of crumbled feta and chilli paste or any of the Peruvian meat dishes you will find later in the book.*

SERVES 4

Flour, for dusting
16–20 small spring roll or wonton
    wrappers
Vegetable or groundnut oil, for frying
1 portion of Amarillo Chilli Sauce
    (see page 232)

FOR THE FILLING

25g fresh white breadcrumbs
100ml evaporated milk
2 tbsp olive oil
1 medium red onion, finely chopped
3 garlic cloves, finely chopped
1 tbsp Amarillo Chilli Paste (see page 226)
150ml Chicken Stock (see page 237)
25g Parmesan cheese, finely grated
1 tbsp ground pecans
320g cooked chicken, shredded
½ tsp ground cumin
A squeeze of lime juice
Salt and freshly ground black pepper

First, make the filling. Soak the breadcrumbs in the evaporated milk. Heat the olive oil in a large frying pan over medium heat and add the onion. Sauté until soft and then add the garlic and Amarillo Chilli Paste. Fry for another few minutes until the paste starts to separate from the oil. Deglaze with the stock, bring to the boil and add the soaked breadcrumbs. Allow the mixture to reduce over medium heat until it is a creamy consistency. Add the Parmesan, pecans and chicken. Season with salt, pepper and cumin, add the lime juice and chill.

To make the rolls, dust your work surface with flour and place about 1 dessertspoon of the chicken mixture horizontally along a spring roll or wonton wrapper – position it quite close to the edge, leaving a 2cm gap at either side. Fold over the wrapper on either side and then roll from the bottom until you have a cylinder. Gently press the roll to make sure the filling is evenly spread. Brush cold water along the edge of the wrapper to seal it, and leave to 'glue' while you make the rest.

If you have a deep-fat fryer, heat the oil to 160°C. If not, pour the oil to a depth of about 5cm in a large, deep saucepan, making sure that it is no more than half full. To test if the oil is hot enough, drop in a cube of bread; if it sizzles and turns golden, the oil is ready.

Fry the rolls in batches, for 3–4 minutes, until a crisp golden brown all over. Drain on kitchen paper and serve immediately with the Amarillo Chilli Sauce.

CHIFLES

DEEP-FRIED PLANTAIN *These are my all-time favourite snack. They are crisp, salty and perfect for eating in front of a good film – and so popular with the kids that that they often don't even make it to the table before they're devoured.*

SERVES 4

4 green plantains
Vegetable oil, for frying
Salt

Peel the plantains and cut them diagonally lengthways into 1mm slices or as thinly as you can. You can also use a potato peeler to achieve a very thin slice.

If you have a deep-fat fryer, heat the vegetable oil to 180°C. If not, pour the oil to a depth of about 5cm in a large, deep saucepan, making sure that it is no more than half full. To test if the oil is hot enough, drop in a cube of bread; if it sizzles and turns golden, the oil is ready.

Fry the plantain slices in the hot oil, turning constantly, until golden brown. Drain on kitchen paper and season with salt. Eat immediately while crispy and hot.

CANCHA

SHALLOW-FRIED CORN *This is a very popular Andean snack, but it's eaten everywhere in Peru. It has a nutty flavour and is incredibly crunchy, not to mention addictive.*

Heat the vegetable oil in a lidded frying pan set over medium heat. Add the corn and fry, shaking frequently until the corn starts to pop. Cover, turn the heat down and cook for about 5 minutes, continuing to shake frequently, until the corn is a deep golden brown with a bit of charring in places.

Tip the corn into a bowl, sprinkle with salt and leave to cool down. This will keep well (at least a couple of weeks) if stored in an airtight container. The corn can be eaten warm or cold with a squeeze of lime juice if you like.

SERVES 4

1 tbsp vegetable oil
250g chulpe corn
1 tsp salt
A squeeze of lime juice (optional)

TAMALES DE QUESO

CHEESE TAMALES *These are the most loved street food in Peru – steamed corn dumplings that are fluffy and very moreish. You can fill them with all kinds of delicious leftovers, stews or casseroles.*

MAKES 4

4 banana leaves or corn husks
4 tbsp cream cheese or Fresh Cheese
   (see page 239)
1 portion of julienned Salsa Criolla
   (see page 236)

FOR THE DOUGH

2 ripe choclo cobs (see page 223)
   or corn-on-the-cobs
50g butter
1 tbsp Amarillo Chilli Paste (see page 226)
3 garlic cloves, crushed
A pinch of salt
A pinch of sugar
2 egg yolks

First, make the dough. Cut the choclo or corn kernels from the cob. Put them in a food processor or blender and add a couple of tablespoons of water. Blitz until smooth.

Melt the butter in a shallow, wide-based saucepan set over medium heat. Add the Amarillo Chilli Paste and the garlic and sauté for 1 minute. Add the blended choclo or corn, season with pinches of salt and sugar and then cook the mixture for about 10 minutes, stirring constantly. After this time the mixture should be dry, smooth and any floury taste from the corn should be cooked out.

Remove the choclo mixture from the saucepan and leave it to cool a little. Add the egg yolks and mix thoroughly. Divide the dough into 4.

To assemble, take a piece of dough and flatten it down to about 5mm thick in the centre of the banana leaf. Put a tablespoon of cheese in the centre of the dough, and then lift up the sides of the leaf to help you wrap the dough around the filling so that the cheese is completely encased. Fold the banana leaf edges over the tamale on all sides to create a roughly square parcel. Tie securely with string and place in a steamer. Repeat for all tamales.

Steam for 30 minutes and then unwrap and serve with the Salsa Criolla.

VARIATION

♦ *Coriander tamales:* a beautiful green version can be made with the addition of Coriander Oil (see page 235). Simply reduce the amount of butter to 10g and replace with 2–3 tablespoons Coriander Oil. You can use the same cheese filling or some shredded meat from either the Duck Confit (see page 109) or the Lamb Braised in Beer (see page 91).

MAMITA'S TAMALES

Tamales always remind me of my grandmother, Mamita Naty. She was a strong Andean woman who worked hard until her last breath. Every few months, my grandmother would send an *encomienda* (hamper) from her village to our family in Lima. It was always full of *queso fresco* (fresh cheese), *jamón de la sierra* (ham), eggs and sometimes even a live hen, cockerel or turkey, but best of all it included my favourite chicken-filled tamales. The only tamales that come close to those made by my grandmother are those made by Doña Maria Zuñigas, who is carrying on the family business set up by her mother over 60 years ago. She makes her own unique tamales using chickpeas, corn and purple maize and fills them with all kinds of ingredients, including pork, chicken, asparagus and cheese.

HUMITAS DULCE

SWEET TAMALES *Because tamales are such a popular street food, they appear in markets all over Peru in both savoury and sweet guises. This recipe for a sweet tamale, uses choclo (pictured right) and are generally steamed in corn husks.*

MAKES 4

50g raisins
4 tbsp pisco
4 tbsp cream cheese or Fresh Cheese
   (see page 239)
4 large corn husks

FOR THE DOUGH

2 ripe choclo cobs (see page 223)
   or corn-on-the-cobs
50ml evaporated milk or single cream
50g butter
2 tsp ground cinnamon
50g light soft brown sugar,
   plus 1 extra tbsp
2 egg yolks

Put the raisins in a saucepan, cover with pisco and add 1 teaspoon of the ground cinnamon. Set over medium heat and bring to the boil. Take off the heat and then leave to infuse while you prepare the tamale dough.

Cut the choclo or corn kernels from the cob. Put them in a food processor or blender and add the evaporated milk or cream. Blitz until smooth.

Melt the butter in a shallow, wide-based saucepan set over medium heat. Add the blended choclo or corn, the remaining ground cinnamon and the 50g sugar and then cook the mixture for about 10 minutes, stirring constantly. After this time the mixture should be dry, smooth and any floury taste from the corn should be cooked out.

Remove the choclo mixture from the saucepan and leave it to cool briefly. Add the egg yolks and mix thoroughly. Divide the dough into 4 portions.

Drain the soaked raisins and transfer to a bowl. Add the cheese and the extra light soft brown sugar and mix well.

To assemble, take a piece of dough and flatten it down to about 5mm thick in the centre of a corn husk. Put a tablespoon of the raisin and cheese mixture in the centre of the dough, and then lift up the sides of the husk to help you wrap the dough around the filling so that the cheese is completely encased. Fold the husk edges over the tamale on all sides to create a neat square parcel. Tie securely with string. Repeat for all tamales. Place in a steamer for 30 minutes and then unwrap and serve.

3
–
FISH

I LOVE THE PACIFIC OCEAN. *This is partly because I love to surf and the Peruvian coastline is a surfer's paradise, but of course I also love it for its fish. When I was a child, my father used to take me to the small fishing village of Pucusana, south of Lima, where we would hire a small boat and take to the sea. Despite the fact that our rods were makeshift, we caught fish after fish; everything from* cojinova *or* pejerrey *to sole and the humble sardine.*

Peruvians feel blessed by the abundance of sea life on their doorstep. Ever since the peoples of pre-Inca times first braved the seas in their reed boats, Peruvians have had a fruitful relationship with the Pacific. There are of course reasons why the fish are so diverse and plentiful; a combination of the cooling Humboldt Current and the warmer El Niño provides the perfect environment for plankton to breed, which in turn provides food for one of the widest varieties of fish and seafood in the world.

Some of the best things to do with fish are the simplest. My fondest food memories involve eating ceviche on a boat, made with fish caught straight from the sea, and then later barbecuing some on the beach using a makeshift coal stove. However, this isn't the whole story. Peruvians are very inventive with their fish and seafood cookery and a myriad of influences shine through, from Parmesan Scallops (see page 70) to the traditional Grilled Fish Parcels (see page 82) from the Amazon.

There are many types of fish commonly eaten in Peru that aren't readily available elsewhere, but none of these dishes are dependent on using a specific variety. At our restaurant we prefer to buy the freshest local and sustainable fish. The recommended fish is just a guide, so feel free to get whatever is freshest on the day. As we have suggested in the ceviche chapter, buy the whole fish if you can, even if you get your fishmonger to fillet it for you. You can then make wonderful stocks with the trimmings or robust and tasty fish soups.

CHUPE DE CAMARONES

PRAWN CHOWDER *This is a particularly good soup for a cold winter's night. It has all the warmth and comforting properties of a classic chowder, but with a kick of Peruvian heat to wake up your taste buds.*

SERVES 4

600g raw shell-on prawns
1 litre Shellfish Stock (see page 237),
   made using the heads and shells
   from the prawns
3 tbsp olive oil
1 large red onion, diced
5 garlic cloves, crushed
2 tbsp Amarillo Chilli Paste (see page 226)
   or 2 tbsp tomato purée
   and 1 finely chopped red chilli
2 tomatoes, peeled, deseeded
   and finely chopped
1 tbsp finely chopped fresh oregano
   or 1 tsp dried oregano,
   plus extra to garnish
50g long-grain rice
1 large floury potato, peeled
   and cut into 2cm cubes
1 choclo cob (see page 223)
   or corn-on-the-cob,
   kernels cut from the cob
100ml single cream or evaporated milk
100g peas
4 eggs
50g Fresh Cheese (see page 239)
   or feta, diced
4 large cooked shell-on prawns, to serve
Salt and freshly ground black pepper

Prepare the prawns. Remove the heads and shells from the prawns and use them to make 1 litre Shellfish Stock as instructed on page 237. Devein the prawns and chill until needed.

Heat the oil in a large, heavy-based saucepan. Add the onion and sauté over low heat for 5 minutes until softened. Add the garlic and sauté for a further minute. Next add the Amarillo Chilli Paste and sauté until the oil and paste start to separate.

Add the tomatoes, oregano, freshly made stock and the rice. Bring to the boil and simmer for about 5 minutes. Add the potato cubes and choclo and simmer for 20 minutes. The starch released from the rice and potato should start to thicken the soup.

Check the soup to test that the rice, potato and choclo are cooked. Add the prawns, cream and peas and keep simmering for 5 minutes.

Meanwhile, poach 4 eggs in a saucepan of boiling water or in an egg poacher.

Season with salt and pepper to taste and add the cheese. Pour into serving bowls and top each bowl with a freshly poached egg, a cooked shell-on prawn and a sprinkling of fresh oregano and serve immediately.

NOTE
♦ Evaporated milk is often used instead of single cream as it adds a sweeter flavour.

SOPA DE CANGREJO

CRAB BROTH *This is a very pure consommé served with crabmeat. If you want a more substantial soup, add finely diced onion, celery, carrot and tomato into the strained broth a few minutes before serving. The flavour of this broth is supposed to be quite intense; in fact, Peruvians often refer to it as 'crab concentrate'.*

SERVES 4

4 large crabs
2 litres cold water
1 red onion, chopped
2 celery sticks, chopped
2 tomatoes, peeled, deseeded and chopped
2 garlic cloves, crushed
2 bay leaves
2 tsp freshly ground black pepper
Lime juice
Salt

Crack the crabs slightly with the blunt edge of a large knife or cleaver. Put the crabs in a large saucepan, cover with the cold water and bring to the boil.

Remove any scum that has formed on the surface and then add all the other ingredients. Simmer over low heat for about 1 hour, making sure that the liquid just covers the crabs.

Taste and add salt. If you think the flavour could be more concentrated, simmer for a further 20 minutes. Strain the soup and reserve all the liquid in the pan. If you wish, remove the crab meat from the crabs and add back into the soup, or crack the crabs into pieces and serve these alongside the soup. Add lime juice and salt to taste.

MI PERU AND THE HUARIQUES OF LIMA

Mi Peru is a legendary hole-in-the-wall restaurant found in the Barranco neighbourhood of Lima. Your first impression will be underwhelming. Queues of people will jostle to find space amongst the old wooden benches that are set out around a few tables. However, you will understand its popularity once you taste their crab broth. Mi Peru is one of the many modest, family-run places scattered around Lima. Each restaurant will have its own speciality. Some serve just one dish, usually based on a family recipe that has been passed down through the generations. We have a word for these places: *huariques*. You will always be able to spot a good one; simply drive around Lima and look for the queues. The longer the queue, the better the food.

SUDADO DE CORVINA Y CONCHITAS

SEA BASS & SCALLOP STEW *The complementary flavours of chilli and soy sauce work brilliantly in this dish. The intensely savoury, well-spiced sauce really brings out the sweetness of the fish, scallops and potatoes.*

Season the scallops and the fish with salt, pepper and lime juice and set aside.

Heat the oil in a large, lidded non-stick pan over medium heat. Add the red onion and sauté until softened and then add the garlic and continue to sauté for another minute or two. Add the Amarillo Chilli Paste and Panca Chilli Paste, stir to mix and then pour in the red wine. Turn up the heat and allow this to bubble furiously and reduce until it is around half the original volume. Add the tomatoes, fish stock and soy sauce, cover and then simmer for a couple of minutes for the flavours to come together.

Add the fish and the cooked new potatoes to the pan and simmer for a couple of minutes until the fish is almost cooked through and then add the scallops. Simmer for another 2 minutes.

Serve the fish and potatoes piping hot with the juice poured over and sprinkled with finely chopped spring onions. This dish is delicious served with rice too.

SERVES 4

8 scallops
4 sea bass fillets (or similar fish fillets)
Juice of 1 lime
2 tbsp olive oil
2 red onions, very thinly sliced
4 garlic cloves, crushed
1 tbsp Amarillo Chilli Paste (see page 226)
1 tbsp Aji Panca Paste (see page 225)
200ml red wine
3 tomatoes, deseeded
    and sliced lengthways
200ml Fish Stock (see page 237) or
    good-quality shop-bought fish stock
1 tbsp soy sauce
8 small new potatoes or equivalent,
    peeled, cooked and halved
1 tbsp finely chopped spring onions
Salt and freshly ground black pepper

CONCHITAS A LA PARMESANA

PARMESAN SCALLOPS *This dish sounds Italian, but it isn't and you won't find it anywhere in Italy, let alone in Parma. Its precise origins are unknown, but today it is one of the most popular dishes on the coast of Peru. If you are unsure about opening and cleaning scallops, your fishmonger will be able to do it for you.*

SERVES 4

12 scallops, in the shell
1 tbsp pisco
Juice of 2 limes, plus wedges to serve
2 garlic cloves, crushed
A dash of Worcestershire sauce
75g butter
30g Cheddar cheese, grated
50g Parmesan cheese, grated
Salt and freshly ground black pepper

Preheat the oven to 180°C (gas mark 4).

First, prepare the scallops. Holding a scallop in one hand with the flat shell facing upwards, slide the blade of a knife in between the two shells. Feel for the membrane that joins the scallop to the shell and cut through it. Lift off the top shell. Pull off the dark frilly membrane and the small black sac. Pull the scallop and roe away from the shell, removing the white ligament that will be attached to the scallop. Rinse the shells, scallop meat and roe thoroughly to remove any sand.

Place each scallop with their roe on a shell. Mix the pisco, lime juice, garlic, Worcestershire sauce and some salt and pepper together in a bowl. Drizzle this mixture evenly over the scallops and then dot with butter. Cover each shell with some Cheddar and then some Parmesan.

Place the scallops onto a baking tray and bake in the preheated oven for 10 minutes or until the scallops are just cooked and the cheese is bubbling and golden. Serve with lime wedges.

CHOROS A LA CHALACA

CALLAO MUSSELS *This colourful dish was invented in Callao, a busy port north of Lima. With its hustle and bustle, Callao is a fascinating place. It's worth exploring the variety of food on offer, even if your ears are ringing with the sound of loud salsa and colourful slang.*

SERVES 4

100g choclo or sweetcorn kernels
1 star anise
1 x 2.5cm cinnamon stick
2 cloves
1 tbsp white wine vinegar
1 tbsp sugar

FOR THE MUSSELS

24 large mussels, cleaned and debearded
250ml white wine
½ red onion, cut into wedges
2 garlic cloves, crushed but left whole
2 tsp black peppercorns

FOR THE SALSA

1 portion of finely diced Salsa Criolla
    (see page 236)
1 tbsp olive oil
1 tbsp finely chopped coriander leaves
Salt and freshly ground black pepper

First, cook the choclo. Put the kernels in a saucepan with the star anise, cinnamon stick, cloves, vinegar and sugar and then pour over enough water to cover. Bring the water to a boil, cover and then cook over medium heat for 10 minutes or until the corn has softened and has a sweet flavour.

While the choclo is cooking, wash and pick over the mussels, scraping off any large barnacles, pulling off the beard and discarding any that don't immediately close when you tap them sharply against a hard surface. Put the mussels in a large saucepan with the wine, onion, garlic and black peppercorns. Put the lid on, bring to the boil and cook for 2 minutes, shaking the pan a couple of times. Drain and discard the liquid and any mussels that haven't opened.

Gently pull the mussels from their shells. Discard one half of each shell and place the mussels back onto the remaining half shell. Leave these to cool.

Make the salsa by combining all the ingredients in a bowl.

To assemble, spoon the salsa over the mussels, garnish each shell with a choclo kernel and serve immediately.

VARIATION

♦ Although most commonly made with mussels, it also works with other types of shelled seafood. Try substituting large clams or even use raw oysters; just make sure that you separate the oyster properly from the half shell and add the dressing moments before serving.

ARROZ CON MARISCOS

SEAFOOD RICE *The combination of a Pacific Ocean full of rich pickings, Spanish influences and heavy rice production in the mid 1800s to feed Chinese migrant workers created the platform for this wonderful Peruvian coastal dish.*

SERVES 4

4 tbsp olive oil
500g large shell-on prawns, peeled
   but heads and shells reserved
100ml white wine
250ml water, Fish Stock (see page 237)
   or good-quality shop-bought fish stock
1 large red onion, finely chopped
1 red pepper, deseeded and finely chopped
5 garlic cloves, crushed
1 tbsp Panca Chilli Paste (see page 226)
1 tsp sweet paprika
1 tsp dried oregano
2 tomatoes, deseeded and finely chopped
1 tbsp pisco
2 bay leaves
200g squid, cleaned and cut into rings
1 portion of Peruvian Rice (see page 136)
10g coriander leaves, roughly chopped
Salt and freshly ground black pepper

Heat 2 tablespoons of the olive oil in a very wide, shallow frying pan over high heat. Add the prawn shells and heads and quickly stir until they change to a deep pink/red colour and start to brown around the edges. Pour over the white wine and allow the mixture to sizzle briefly. Add the water or stock, cover and simmer over very low heat for 5 minutes. Strain, reserve the liquor and discard the prawn shells.

Without washing the frying pan, heat the remaining olive oil over medium heat. Add the onion and red pepper and sauté until the onion is translucent and then add the garlic and cook for a further minute.

Add the Panca Chilli Paste, paprika, oregano and tomatoes and stir until everything is coated in the spices. Pour over the reserved prawn liquor and the pisco. Add the bay leaves and season well with salt and pepper. Bring to the boil and then turn down the heat and leave to simmer for 5 minutes. Add the prawns and squid and simmer for a minute longer.

Stir in all of the cooked rice. When the rice is piping hot, serve with roughly torn coriander leaves sprinkled on top.

VARIATION
♦ You can always vary the seafood used in this dish according to what's available. Try it with mussels or clams, or a mixture of these.

JALEA

FRIED SEAFOOD *This simple yet delicious dish uses some typical Peruvian spices to enhance the flavour of the fish.*

Mix all the ingredients for the mayonnaise together in a bowl and set aside until needed.

Season all of the fish and seafood with lime juice, salt and pepper. Put the cornflour and all the spices into a bowl and mix thoroughly. Toss all of the seafood in the flour mixture and tap gently to dust off any excess seasoning.

If you have a deep-fat fryer, heat the oil to 170°C. If not, pour the oil to a depth of about 5cm in a large, deep saucepan, making sure that it is no more than half full. To test if the oil is hot enough, drop in a cube of bread; if it sizzles and turns golden, the oil is ready.

Cook the fish, prawns and squid for 1 minute until the flour coating turns a golden brown. Remove and drain on kitchen paper. The fish and seafood will be slightly crisp but still very juicy inside.

Arrange the fried fish and seafood on serving plates or on a large platter. Sprinkle over the Salsa Criolla and serve with lime wedges for squeezing and the rocoto mayonnaise in a bowl on the side for dipping.

SERVES 4

400g white fish fillets, cut into goujons
12 large raw prawns, peeled
150g squid, sliced into rings
Juice of 1 lime, plus 1 lime,
    cut into wedges, to serve
100g cornflour
1 tsp ground cumin
¼ tsp dried panca chilli, ground
½ tsp paprika
Vegetable oil, for frying
1 portion of julienned Salsa Criolla
    (see page 236)
Salt and freshly ground black pepper

FOR THE ROCOTO MAYONNAISE

100g mayonnaise
2 tsp Rocoto Chilli Paste (see page 226)
½ garlic clove, crushed
A squeeze of lime juice

PULPO AL OLIVO

OCTOPUS IN OLIVE SAUCE *This dish is all about the pairing of two very interesting ingredients: Peruvian botija olives, which have been cured in brine and give the sauce its unique, purple hue; and beautifully cooked octopus.*

Put the octopus in a saucepan along with the garlic, bay leaf and peppercorns. Cover with a lid and simmer over medium heat for about 1 hour until tender.

Remove the octopus from the heat, drain off the cooking liquid and leave to cool down. If you have time, chill the octopus for a short while as it is easier to cut when firmed up a little. Cut the tentacles into thin slices.

To serve, divide the octopus between serving plates. Drizzle with the Olive Sauce, season and then garnish with a few drops of olive oil and a sprinkling of capers and parsley.

SERVES 4

1 small octopus, weighing 700g–1kg, cleaned
2 garlic cloves, crushed
1 bay leaf
½ tsp black peppercorns
½ portion Olive Sauce (see page 234)
3 tbsp extra virgin olive oil
2 tbsp small salted capers, rinsed
2 tbsp finely chopped flat-leaf parsley
Salt and freshly ground black pepper

ESCABECHE DE PESCADO

HOT MARINATED FISH *This dish is a favourite of the great Peruvian singer Susana Baca. It can be eaten cold but I prefer it hot. The sweet potatoes and choclo make this a meal in itself, but you could also serve it on its own as a starter.*

Season the fish with salt and pepper and then dust it with flour. Coat the base of a frying pan with vegetable oil and heat over medium heat. Fry the fish fillets for 2 minutes on each side until golden brown.

Remove the fish from the frying pan. Add the olive oil, turn the heat up and add the red onions, garlic and amarillo chillies. Fry until they have softened and started to take on a bit of colour. Add the tomatoes, cook for a further minute and then add the vinegar and Amarillo Chilli Paste. Add the stock and bay leaf and bring to the boil. Season with sugar, oregano, cumin, salt and black pepper if necessary.

Return the fish to the frying pan and warm through in the sauce. Transfer to serving plates, spooning the sauce over the fish along with plenty of vegetables. This dish is also good served with hard-boiled eggs, Peruvian botija olives, crisp green lettuce and cooked choclo cobs.

SERVES 4

4 large fish fillets, such as coley or hake

Plain flour, for dusting

Vegetable oil, for frying

3 tbsp olive oil

2 red onions, thinly sliced

2 garlic cloves, finely chopped

2 amarillo chillies, sliced into 5mm strips

2 tomatoes, deseeded
    and cut into 2cm slices

50ml red wine vinegar

2 tbsp Amarillo Chilli Paste (see page 226)

50ml Fish Stock (see page 237) or
    good-quality shop-bought fish stock

1 bay leaf

1 tsp caster sugar

1 tsp dried oregano

1 tsp ground cumin

Salt and freshly ground black pepper

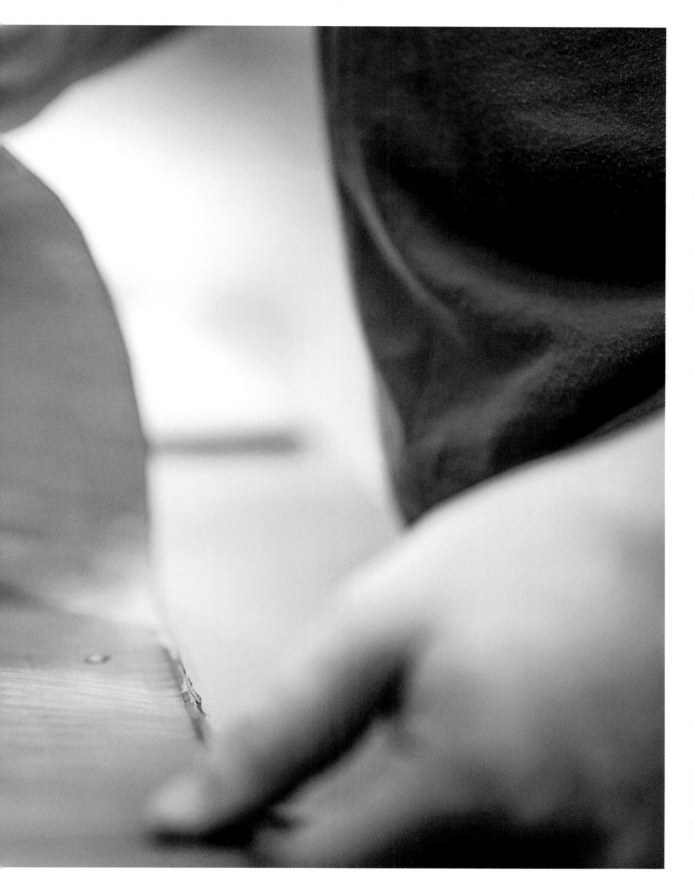

PATARASHCA

GRILLED FISH PARCELS *A traditional dish from the Amazon region of Peru. You can use fish fillets or steaks instead of whole fish if you prefer, just allow roughly a 200g piece per person. This dish is best barbecued outdoors over hot embers, but if that isn't practical, use a griddle pan instead.*

SERVES 4

4 small- to medium-sized white fish
    (sea bream or sea bass are ideal),
    descaled, gutted and cleaned
1 tsp ground cumin
2 red onions, thinly sliced
4 garlic cloves, crushed
4 amarillo chillies, finely chopped
1 small bunch of coriander,
    leaves finely chopped
Vegetable oil
4 banana leaves, for wrapping
Salt and freshly ground black pepper

Score shallow slits into the fish skin on both sides. Season the fish inside and out with salt, pepper and the cumin. Mix the red onions, garlic, chillies and coriander in a bowl and then use it to rub on the sides of each fish and stuff the cavities. Drizzle a teaspoon of vegetable oil over each fish.

Wrap the fish in the banana leaves and secure with string or a skewer if necessary.

Heat your barbecue or griddle pan. When hot, place the parcels on the hot coals or griddle and cook for 20 minutes – this will create an oven effect inside the parcels, enabling the fish to cook. The fish within should still be moist and just cooked through. Serve with boiled or fried cassava.

FISH FROM THE AMAZON

The Amazonian Rainforest is renowned for being one of the most dense and impenetrable places in the world, so it is not surprising that it holds a fascination for Peruvian chefs who are turning to it as a source of new, exciting and exotic ingredients. The Amazon River itself has much to offer; chefs take all kinds of freshwater fish back to Lima, from river snails the size of your hand and giant frogs the size of your feet to *paiche*, a giant freshwater fish. Ceviche in London was the first restaurant in the UK to serve sustainably farmed *paiche*. This unique fish is considered to be the new black cod by chefs around the world. *Patarashca* is probably one of the oldest methods of cooking fish from the Amazon and is commonly made with *paiche* or *tambaqui*.

4
-
MEAT

SOME OF MY MOST VIVID CHILDHOOD MEMORIES *surrounding food involve meat. My mother loved preparing chicken soup, my grandmother bred guinea pigs and my grandfather reared poultry. He also kept a cockerel as a pet that he was very fond of and that he claimed talked to him! My grandparents would often supply us with a live turkey, which would be sent from the mountains to Lima and fed up with pisco in time for Christmas.*

I loved going to the Lince market in Lima with my great-aunties Carmela and Otilia where chickens would be completely free range, running around stallholders' feet. We'd select our animal and return a few minutes later to find it prepared and ready to cook; a far cry from the shrink-wrapped supermarket meat we find today.

Peruvians eat a wide range of different meats. Poultry such as turkey and duck, guinea pig (with a flavour reminiscent of pork and rabbit combined) and alpaca all pre-date the conquistadors and are still very popular. Many traditional dishes have also been adapted to incorporate meat from animals brought by the Spanish, such as sheep, goats, cattle, chicken and, best of all, pigs. One of the earliest exchanges of food between indigenous Peruvians and the Spanish was potato and maize for pork.

Meat has always been a luxury. Indigenous Peruvians and Africans were especially good at making the most of the cheaper cuts that were available. They made anticuchos, *which saw them use ox heart instead of beef, and they also cooked* guisos *(stews) frequently made from offal. All of their dishes of course were enhanced by the spices they had at their disposal.*

The meat dishes I have included here are among my favourites, with some inspired by the classics and some that are imbued with great memories, history and stories – from Andean dishes such as our much-loved Lomo Saltado *recipe and Fibbing Guinea Pig (using rabbit) to Chinese-Peruvian* chifa *stir-fries and French-inspired Duck Confit with Green Rice.*

LOMO SALTADO

PERUVIAN BEEF STIR-FRY *This is not just Peru's most popular stir-fry; it is a perfect fusion of east and west thanks to the combination of Chinese soy, Peruvian chilli and pisco.*

SERVES 4

600g fillet steak, cut into 3cm cubes
Vegetable oil, for frying
1 large red onion, cut into thick wedges
2 tomatoes, halved, deseeded
   and cut lengthways into eighths
1 amarillo chilli, deseeded
   and sliced lengthways
20ml pisco
25g coriander leaves, finely chopped
10g flat-leaf parsley, finely chopped

FOR THE MARINADE

4 garlic cloves, chopped
150ml soy sauce
30ml red wine vinegar
2 tsp Worcestershire sauce
½ tsp dried oregano
½ tsp ground cumin
2 tbsp water
Salt and freshly ground black pepper

Make the marinade by mixing all the ingredients together in a bowl. Add the meat to the bowl and mix so that it is well covered in marinade. Leave to marinate in the fridge for about 4 hours.

Drain the meat, reserving the marinade. Heat the vegetable oil in a wok over high heat until just smoking and then add the meat – be careful, the oil might splutter at you. Cook as quickly as possible, tossing it until the meat is browned on all sides.

Add the red onion and cook for 1 minute. Add the tomatoes and chilli and immediately pour in the pisco.

Pour over the reserved marinade, turn off the heat and leave the meat to rest in the sauce for a couple of minutes. Garnish with chopped coriander and parsley. Serve this dish with thick-cut chips and white rice as traditionally served in Peru.

NOTE

♦ To add some extra smokiness you could also flambé the meat and vegetables as you pour in the pisco. To do this, *very carefully* tilt the pan into the gas flame to invite it into the pan and stir vigorously. If you don't have a gas flame, just follow the above instructions and ensure that the pan is as hot as possible before you add any ingredients.

IN SEARCH OF THE PERFECT LOMO SALTADO

There are countless recipes for *lomo saltado*, but we think that our version at Ceviche can compete with the best of them. Before Ceviche opened, I went to Peru on a mission. In seven days, I visited 27 restaurants; everywhere from fine-dining establishments to hole-in-the-wall restaurants, and tried the *lomo saltado* in every single one. I watched how each one was prepared, saw the ingredients and equipment used and, above all, tasted, tasted, tasted. Then I brought back everything I had learned to London, designed the kitchen around our wok and, with our head chef, finally came up with this great recipe. The effort paid off as it's now one of our best-loved dishes.

SECO DE CABRITO

LAMB BRAISED IN BEER WITH CORIANDER *A classic dish from northern Peru that has a delicious combination of flavours. The sauce has a little heat and the flavour of coriander dominates, but it is tempered perfectly by the sweetness of the peas and potatoes.*

Heat the oil in a large saucepan or flameproof casserole over medium heat. Add the meat, and brown well on all sides. Remove from the casserole. Add the red onion and sauté until soft and then add the garlic and cook for a further minute. Return the meat to the casserole along with the chilli and the cumin. Season with salt and pepper.

Put the bunch of coriander and the citrus juice in a food processor or blender and blitz to a paste, adding a little water if necessary. Add two-thirds of this to the meat, along with the beer. Cover, bring to the boil and then simmer over low heat until the meat is very tender – this should take at least 1½–2 hours.

Add the potatoes and red pepper and cook for a further 20 minutes. Add the peas and simmer until they are soft and until much of the liquid has evaporated. Stir in the remaining coriander mixture.

Serve with steaming hot white rice.

NOTES

♦ Lamb, mutton and kid goat are used fairly interchangeably in Peru. If you do use mutton or kid goat you will need to add a further 30–40 minutes to the cooking time.

♦ Use Peruvian Cusqueña beer if you can. It has the perfect balance of flavours and you can always sneak a sip while you are cooking!

SERVES 4

3 tbsp vegetable oil

1kg lamb (mixture of leg and shoulder), cut into large chunks

1 large red onion, thinly sliced

3 garlic cloves, crushed

1 amarillo chilli, deseeded and chopped

1 tsp ground cumin

1 large bunch of coriander, roughly chopped

Juice of 1 lime or Seville orange

250ml beer (see Note)

500g new or small waxy potatoes, peeled

1 red pepper, deseeded and thinly sliced

250g peas

Salt and freshly ground black pepper

ESCABECHE DE SANGRECITA

MARINATED BLACK PUDDING & VEGETABLES *A dish created by chef Gregor Funcke, it is a loose adaptation of the much-loved dish* sangrecita, *made from chickens' blood, which has been eaten for centuries in Peru. Here we use black pudding and add some new spices and touches of creativity.*

Heat the oil over medium heat in a shallow saucepan wide enough to hold all the black pudding comfortably in one layer – but do not add the black pudding yet.

Add the onions to the oil and sauté over medium heat for 5–10 minutes or until the onions begin to colour. Add the garlic, amarillo chillies and tomatoes and sauté gently for a further minute.

Pour in the red wine vinegar, bring to the boil and immediately turn down to a low heat. Add the stock, sugar, cumin, oregano and some salt and black pepper. Stir gently until the sugar has completely dissolved.

Add the slices of black pudding to the sauce in one single layer. Cover, and leave to simmer over the lowest possible heat for about 10 minutes. This needs to be done very slowly, otherwise the black pudding will break up.

Carefully arrange the black pudding on plates with the Orange-glazed Sweet Potato and spoon any liquid from the pan over the top. Garnish with some coriander leaves.

SERVES 4

3 tbsp olive oil
2 red onions, thinly sliced
1 garlic clove, finely chopped
2 amarillo chillies, deseeded and julienned
2 tomatoes, deseeded and cut into eighths
1 tbsp red wine vinegar
100ml Chicken Stock (see page 237) or good-quality shop-bought chicken stock
1 tsp granulated sugar
½ tsp ground cumin
1 tsp dried oregano
400g black pudding, sliced into 1.5cm rounds
Salt and freshly ground black pepper

TO SERVE

1 portion Orange-glazed Sweet Potato (see page 131)
A few coriander leaves, roughly torn

SHAMBAR

HAM & BEAN SOUP *In northern Peru, this soup used to be called 'Monday Soup', as it was known to give farmers and workers strength at the start of the week. It's quite a thin broth, but the presence of chickpeas and beans means it is very sustaining and filling.*

SERVES 4

100g wheat berries (or pearled barley
   or spelt)
100g pinto beans
100g chickpeas
1 small ham hock, weighing 750g–1kg
2 bay leaves
2 garlic cloves, crushed
1 large onion, chopped
200g fresh or frozen broad beans
A small bunch of coriander and mint
Salt and freshly ground black pepper

Soak the wheat berries, pinto beans and chickpeas overnight in separate bowls of water. The following day, put the ham hock in a large saucepan and cover it with cold water. Bring it to the boil over medium heat. Leave for 1 minute and then drain, washing the hock under cold water. Cover again with cold water, add the bay leaves, garlic and the onion and return to the boil. Reduce the heat and simmer for about 30 minutes.

Put the chickpeas, pinto beans and wheat berries into a separate saucepan. Cover with water, bring to the boil and then drain, discarding the water. Refill the saucepan with water and bring back to the boil. Allow to boil over medium heat for about 30 minutes. Drain and then put the pulses and grains into the same saucepan as the ham hock and continue simmering over low to medium heat for about 30 minutes.

Add the broad beans and continue cooking for 30 minutes until the beans and pulses are just tender. Be careful not to overcook as you do not want the pulses to disintegrate into the liquid. Top up with water from time to time if necessary, as you want a fairly liquid broth.

Remove the ham hock from the soup, discard the bone and skin and flake the meat into large chunks. Return the meat to the soup.

Season to taste and then stir in the herbs. Leave to stand for a few minutes to cool just a little before serving.

CARAPULCRA

ANDEAN PORK & POTATO CASSEROLE *Traditionally made in clay pots, this is said to be one of the oldest Peruvian dishes. Some Peruvian restaurants still use clay pots to make this, but an earthenware or cast-iron casserole will work just as well.*

Preheat the oven to 150°C (gas mark 2).

Heat a frying pan over medium heat and toast the Andean Dehydrated Potato until lightly browned. Transfer to a bowl and cover with water. Leave to soak for about 30 minutes.

Mix all the marinade ingredients together in a bowl or jug and pour over the diced pork in a shallow bowl. Leave to marinate for at least 30 minutes, preferably slightly longer.

Heat the vegetable oil in a large casserole dish over medium heat and sauté the pork until browned on all sides. Remove the pork with a slotted spoon and set aside. Add the chopped onion and any of the remaining marinade along with the cumin and black pepper and sauté until the onion has softened. Deglaze the pan with the white wine and then return the meat to the pan. Drain the potatoes and add them to the casserole (or add the new potatoes if using). Pour over the stock, season with salt and cover with a lid.

Cook the casserole in the preheated oven for 1½ hours. Add the peanuts, port and chocolate and then return to the oven to cook uncovered for another 30 minutes until the sauce has thickened. Remove from the oven and serve with Peruvian Rice (see page 136).

NOTE

♦ The Andean Dehydrated Potatoes do have a distinctive, more intense flavour than fresh potatoes so it is worth trying them. Otherwise, substitute the dried potatoes with 750g small waxy potatoes and sauté them after the pork.

SERVES 4

250g Andean Dehydrated Potatoes (see page 240) or 750g small waxy potatoes (see Note)
750g pork, cut into 3cm chunks
2 tbsp vegetable oil
1 onion, finely chopped
1 tbsp ground cumin
½ tsp freshly ground black pepper
100ml white wine
250ml Chicken Stock (see page 237) or good-quality shop-bought chicken stock
50g roasted peanuts, ground
2 tbsp port
10g dark chocolate, chopped
Salt

FOR THE MARINADE

4 garlic cloves, crushed
1 tbsp Panca Chilli Paste (see page 226)
1 tbsp Amarillo Chilli Paste (see page 226)
50ml red wine vinegar

COSTILLAS CON SAUCO

PORK RIBS WITH ELDERBERRY SAUCE *In Peru, elderberries have the perfect combination of tartness and sweetness and can even be eaten raw (their European cousins are much tarter). Use them to make Elderberry Jelly (see page 242) that can then go on to be added to the wonderfully rich and sticky sauce for these moreish pork ribs.*

Preheat the oven to 200°C (gas mark 6).

Mix the butter, soy sauce and garlic together in a bowl and season with some salt and pepper. Spread this over the ribs making sure they are well covered and then put them into a roasting dish. Roast in the preheated oven for about 1 hour, basting and turning regularly, until they have deepened in colour to a rich brown. They should still be very juicy. Remove from the oven and leave to rest while you make the sauce.

To make the sauce: heat a frying pan over medium heat and dry-fry the bacon until fat renders out and until it is crisp and browned. Remove from the heat and set aside.

Melt the Elderberry Jelly in a small saucepan over medium heat and then add the red wine and the bacon. Bring to the boil and then simmer the sauce until it has darkened and reduced to a syrupy consistency. Taste for seasoning and add salt, pepper and the sugar if you think it needs it.

Pour any juices from the resting cooked ribs into the sauce and heat for a minute longer. Serve the ribs with generous amounts of the sauce poured over the top.

SERVES 4

50g butter, melted
50ml soy sauce
2 garlic cloves, crushed
1kg meaty, fat pork ribs
Salt and freshly ground black pepper

FOR THE SAUCE
200g smoked bacon lardons
250g Elderberry Jelly (see page 242)
250ml red wine
1 tbsp caster sugar

POLLO DE MI TÍA CARMELA

CARMELA'S CHICKEN *My great-aunt Carmela often made this for Sunday lunch when my family visited, served with rice or spaghetti, a generous helping of Salsa Criolla (see page 236) and some homemade chilli sauce. I love to mash an avocado with salt and pepper and mix it with the chicken for added creaminess.*

Heat the olive oil in a deep, wide saucepan over medium heat. Add the chicken pieces and fry until browned all over. As you turn the chicken pieces, season the cooked side with some salt, pepper and half the cumin. Once all sides are a deep, golden brown, remove the chicken from the pan.

Add the onions and carrots to the pan and fry until lightly caramelised. Add the garlic and cook for a couple more minutes and then add the tomatoes. Turn up the heat slightly and cook for a few more minutes until the tomatoes have broken down and some of their juices have evaporated. Return the chicken to the pan, sprinkle over the remaining cumin and pour over the stock. Bring to the boil and then turn the heat down and simmer for 45 minutes until the sauce is reduced and the meat is almost falling off the bone.

Cook the spaghetti according to the packet instructions until cooked. Drain in a colander and return to the saucepan. Strain off a ladleful of the chicken liquor and mix it with the pasta and then divide the pasta between 4 large shallow bowls. Add the rest of the chicken and sauce. The avocado is optional. If you like, mash a ripe avocado up in a small bowl and season with salt and pepper. Mix it in with the chicken and pasta.

SERVES 4

2 tbsp olive oil

4 chicken legs or 8 thighs

1 tsp cumin

1 large red onion, very finely chopped

2 carrots, grated

2 garlic cloves, crushed

4 large tomatoes, skinned, deseeded and
   very finely chopped

300ml Chicken Stock (see page 237) or
   good-quality shop-bought chicken stock

350g dried spaghetti

1 ripe avocado (optional)

Salt and freshly ground black pepper

POLLO SALTADO

CHICKEN & CRISPY POTATO STIR-FRY *This is one of many dishes made popular by the Chinese-Peruvian-run* chifa *restaurants found in the largest cities of Peru.*

SERVES 4

2 chicken breasts, cut into thin strips

2–3 tbsp vegetable oil, plus extra for frying

1 large red onion, thinly sliced lengthways

1 large red pepper, deseeded
   and thinly sliced lengthways

3 tomatoes, deseeded and cut into eighths

2 garlic cloves, crushed

450g potatoes, peeled
   and cut into chunky chips

2 spring onions, cut into thirds lengthways
   and then shredded

A few coriander leaves, roughly torn

Salt and freshly ground black pepper

FOR THE MARINADE

1 tbsp soy sauce

1 tbsp red wine or rice vinegar

Juice of ½ a lime

1 tsp ground cumin

1 tbsp Panca Chilli Paste (see page 226)

Mix the marinade ingredients together in a bowl and add the chicken. Mix thoroughly, cover, and leave to marinate for a few hours, but preferably overnight.

Put the oil in a wok and place over medium to high heat until hot and slightly smoking. Drain the chicken, reserving the marinade juices. Add the chicken to the wok and brown on all sides and then pour over the reserved marinade. Cook for 2–3 minutes, stirring constantly, until the chicken is cooked through.

Remove the chicken from the wok with a slotted spoon and set aside. Add a little more vegetable oil to the wok. Heat it again and then add the red onion and red pepper. Fry, stirring constantly for a few minutes until they start to soften and brown around the edges. Add the tomatoes and garlic and cook until the tomatoes have started to soften.

Return the chicken to the wok and taste for seasoning – you may want to add more soy sauce, lime juice or chilli.

Meanwhile, make the chips. If you have a deep-fat fryer, heat the oil to 160°C. If not, pour the oil to a depth of about 5cm in a large, deep saucepan, making sure that it is no more than half full. To test if the oil is hot enough, drop in a cube of bread; if it sizzles and turns golden, the oil is ready. Cook the chips until softened but not taking on colour. Turn the heat up slightly (to 190°C if using a deep-fat fryer) and fry for a couple more minutes until golden brown. Drain thoroughly on kitchen paper.

To assemble, add the chips to the wok and gently turn everything over so that they take on some of the flavour. Serve in shallow bowls with a garnish of shredded spring onions and roughly torn coriander leaves. This dish goes very well with Peruvian Rice (see page 136).

CHIFAS & CHINESE-PERUVIAN CUISINE

The history of Chinese migration to Peru hasn't always been
a happy one, but it has produced exceptional food and flavour
combinations. After the abolition of slavery in the mid 1850s,
many Chinese workers were brought in as cheap labour.
One of the few ways they were able to keep their links to
their homeland was through food; the ingredients weren't the
same, but the methods were, and the tradition of wok-cooked
Peruvian food was born. Many of these Chinese workers set up
restaurants in Capon Street in Lima. This is where the first *chifas*
(from the Mandarin phrase *chi fan* meaning 'eat rice, eat meal')
were opened. Some also say that the word *chifa* comes from the
Chinese *nichi fan* or 'have you eaten yet?' There are now over
20,000 *chifas* in Peru, all serving Cantonese-Peruvian dishes.

POLLO CON COLA

COCA-COLA CHICKEN *This is one of the simplest recipes that my great-aunt Otilia used to make. She claimed the recipe was her own invention although I suspect its origins came from the local* chifa *restaurants that served versions of sweet-and-sour chicken – wherever it came from, she had improvised it brilliantly.*

SERVES 4

1 chicken, jointed into pieces, or 8 thigh
and/or drumstick portions
250ml Coca-Cola (not the diet variety)
60ml soy sauce
2 tbsp Chinese five-spice powder
1 tsp cumin
1 large onion, finely chopped
4 garlic cloves, finely chopped
Salt and freshly ground black pepper

Preheat the oven to 200°C (gas mark 6). Arrange the chicken pieces in a roasting dish.

Mix all the other ingredients together in a bowl and pour over the chicken. Cover with foil and bake in the preheated oven for about 30 minutes, basting with the juices after 15 minutes. Remove the foil and baste again. If it looks slightly too dry and in danger of burning, add a tablespoon or so of water to the roasting dish as well. Return to the oven for another 15–20 minutes, until the chicken has a slightly sticky, crispy skin and the sauce has reduced to a syrup.

Serve with the sauce spooned over, with freshly cooked white rice and some greens or fried cassava.

GREAT-AUNTS OTILIA & CARMELA

Between the 1950s and 70s, my great-aunts (both spinsters and devout Catholics) brought up my mother and her six siblings in the working-class neighbourhood of Lince; my grandparents remained in the mountains of Cachicadan. My great-aunts were tireless; despite juggling child-rearing with full-time jobs, they loved to entertain at their house. Parties always involved food and any excuse was given for holding a banquet. I owe my love of cooking, entertaining and hospitality to them. They were always generous and welcoming to friends, neighbours and especially, of course, family.

PAVO NAVIDEÑO

CHRISTMAS TURKEY *We love suckling pig and sometimes even duck at Christmas, but generally in Peru we prefer turkey. Internationally, there are many classic Christmas turkey recipes, but this Peruvian version is unique and full of flavour.*

SERVES 6–8

1 small turkey, weighing about 4kg
1 large onion, cut into thick slices
250ml water
1–2 tbsp plain flour

FOR THE BRINE

6 litres water
125g salt
125ml honey
4 tbsp black peppercorns, lightly crushed
2 large cinnamon sticks
1 large bunch of rosemary
4 bay leaves, crumbled
Zest and juice of 2 oranges

FOR THE STUFFING

25g butter
1 onion, finely chopped
2 garlic cloves, finely chopped
50g raisins
50ml pisco
200g white breadcrumbs
50g pecans, crumbled
2 carrots, grated
2 apples, peeled and diced
50ml single cream

(continued on page 106)

Put all the brine ingredients into your largest stockpot or clean bucket and stir until the salt, sugar and honey has dissolved. Submerge your turkey; if the water doesn't completely cover it, add a bit more. Leave it for at least a day somewhere cold (an unheated garage is ideal). Remove the turkey from the brine and pat dry. Leave to return to room temperature (the water will have kept it quite cold) while you make the stuffing.

Preheat the oven to 200°C (gas mark 6).

To make the stuffing: melt the butter in a frying pan over medium heat and add the onion. Sauté until the onion is soft and translucent and then add the garlic. Cook for another couple of minutes and then set aside and leave to cool completely. Put the raisins and pisco in a very small saucepan and heat through until bubbling and the alcohol has been cooked away. Set aside to cool. Mix the onions and garlic with the rest of the stuffing ingredients, including the pisco-infused raisins. Weigh this mixture, as you will need to add this to the weight of the turkey to work out the overall cooking time. Put the stuffing into both ends of the turkey.

Next, make the basting sauce. Melt the butter in a saucepan over medium heat. Remove from the heat and add in all the other ingredients for the basting sauce.

Spread the onion slices on the bottom of a large roasting tin and place the stuffed turkey on top. Baste the turkey generously with the sauce, keeping some back for extra basting during the roasting process.

FOR THE BASTING SAUCE

50g butter
1 tbsp Dijon mustard
Juice of 1 lime
Juice of 1 orange
50ml soy sauce
50ml pisco

Roast the turkey in the preheated oven for 30 minutes. Remove from the oven and baste again adding 250ml water to the roasting tin. Turn the temperature down to 160°C (gas mark 3). Cook for 30 minutes for each kilogram (including the weight of the stuffing as mentioned earlier) remembering to baste with the cooking juices regularly. It is done when the juices in the thigh run clear, or test with a meat thermometer in the thickest part of the bird – it should be 74°C.

Remove the turkey from the oven and transfer to a large serving plate. Cover with foil and leave to rest for 20 minutes while you make the gravy.

To make the gravy, pour all the cooking juices from the roasting tin into a jug and spoon off all the fat from the surface. Remove the onion from the roasting tin (eating this is a chef's perk!). Place the roasting tin over low heat. Sprinkle in the flour and stir, scraping up any sticky bits from the bottom; you should end up with a roux-like mixture. Gradually add the cooking juices until you have a rich, brown gravy. Taste for seasoning and adjust accordingly. Carve the turkey meat and serve with the gravy and stuffing.

NOTE

♦ To serve with a very simple turmeric rice salad: cook 400g rice in water with 1 teaspoon of turmeric. Drain, cool, then toss with freshly chopped green and red pepper, ½ a red onion and a small handful of raisins.

CHRISTMAS IN PERU

As you would expect from a country which is 81 per cent Catholic, there are many traditions and spectacles attached to Christmas, from the colourful altarpieces of Ayacucho to the lively Afro-Peruvian parades in El Carmen. Many traditions are food related – such as having adopted the traditional Christmas dinner – and are quite cosmopolitan. For example, alongside turkey, *tamales* are eaten, and Peruvians also eat almost 20 million Italian panettones every Christmas!

AGUADITO

TURKEY & RICE SOUP *This economical soup makes good use of any stock made from leftover turkey carcasses. Comforting and nourishing, it is also a renowned hangover cure.*

Heat the olive oil in a large saucepan over medium heat and add the onion. Sauté gently for 10–15 minutes or until the onion is translucent and softened. Add the garlic, chilli and carrots and cook for a further 2 minutes.

Add the stock and potatoes and season with salt and pepper. Add the choclo kernels and rice to the pot and cook over a low heat, slightly covered, for about 20 minutes. Add the red pepper and peas and cook for a further 10 minutes. Add the turkey reserved from the stock, making sure it is quite finely shredded. Check for seasoning and then add the pisco and lime juice as necessary and allow it to warm through for a few minutes. Serve in large shallow soup bowls.

SERVES 4

2 tbsp olive oil

1 onion, finely chopped

2 garlic cloves, crushed

1 amarillo chilli, finely chopped

3 carrots, peeled and sliced

1.5 litres Turkey or Chicken Stock
   (see page 237) and reserved meat, or
   good-quality shop-bought chicken stock

2 small peeled potatoes, cut into quarters

2 large choclo cobs (see page 223)
   or corn-on-the-cobs, kernels cut
   from the cobs

100g long-grain rice

1 red pepper, cut into strips

200g peas, fresh or frozen

1 tbsp pisco

Juice of ½ a lime, to taste

Salt and freshly ground black pepper

ARROZ CON PATO

CONFIT DUCK WITH GREEN RICE *Start this recipe at least a day before you want to eat it, as the duck is marinated overnight and then heated gently in oil. If you are in a hurry you could use shop-bought duck confit and just add some orange zest to the sauce.*

Rub the duck legs with orange zest, chopped garlic, salt and olive oil. Leave in the fridge overnight to marinate.

The next day, preheat the oven to 150°C (gas mark 2). Brush the marinade off the duck legs, taking particular care to get rid of the garlic, and put the duck in a casserole dish. Cover the duck with the vegetable oil, completely immersing them. Cook in the preheated oven for 2 hours until the meat is soft, but not brown, and has started to fall away from the bone. Remove the casserole from the oven and carefully strain the hot fat away – be careful as it will be very hot and is likely to spit and splutter. Carefully remove the bone from the meat, keeping the skin and meat intact.

To make the sauce, first put the coriander, parsley and half the peas in a food processor or blender and blitz to a thick green paste, adding water if necessary.

Heat the olive oil in a large saucepan and sauté the onion, garlic and pepper until they begin to soften. Add the Amarillo Chilli Paste and cook for a further minute. Deglaze the saucepan with the beer and bring to the boil. Add the stock and half the green paste. Simmer and reduce for 5 minutes. Season with the cumin, orange juice, sugar, salt and pepper. Taste and find a balance between the heat of the chilli, the bitterness of the beer and the sweetness of the orange.

Add the Peruvian Rice, remaining peas, choclo or sweetcorn and the rest of the green paste. Stir until heated through.

Heat an ovenproof heavy-based frying pan with a dash of oil over high heat and sauté the cooked duck meat, skin side down, until the skin is brown and crispy on all sides.

Check for seasoning and then serve the rice in large dishes with the duck legs on top. Garnish with some Salsa Criolla.

SERVES 4

4 duck legs
Vegetable oil, to confit
1 portion of Peruvian Rice (see page 136) made with 320g long-grain rice
50g choclo (see page 223) or sweetcorn
1 portion of Salsa Criolla (see page 236)
Salt and freshly ground black pepper

FOR THE MARINADE

Zest of 1 orange
1 garlic clove, finely chopped
1 tsp salt
2 tbsp olive oil

FOR THE SAUCE

1 bunch of coriander (about 100g, including stems)
½ bunch of flat-leaf parsley (about 50g, including stems)
300g fresh peas
2 tbsp olive oil
1 red onion, finely diced
2 garlic cloves, crushed
1 red pepper, deseeded and finely diced
½ tbsp Amarillo Chilli Paste (see page 226)
250ml Guinness (or other beer or stout)
250ml Chicken Stock (see page 237) or good-quality shop-bought chicken stock
A pinch of cumin
Juice of 1 orange
A pinch of caster sugar

PICANTE DE CUY MENTIROSO

FIBBING GUINEA PIG *For this recipe we've used rabbit instead of guinea pig, hence its cheeky name. Eating guinea pig may seem a little strange to some. However, in Andean regions, guinea pigs have been domesticated as livestock for thousands of years.*

SERVES 4

1 rabbit, weighing 1½–2kg, jointed
2 tbsp olive oil
1 red onion, finely chopped
1 tbsp Amarillo Chilli Paste (see page 226)
1 tbsp Panca Chilli Paste (see page 226)
100ml white wine
250ml Chicken Stock (see page 237) or
    good-quality shop-bought chicken stock
50g roasted peanuts, ground
12 new potatoes
1 tbsp finely chopped flat-leaf parsley
Salt and freshly ground black pepper

FOR THE MARINADE
4 garlic cloves, crushed
1 tbsp cumin
1 tsp dried oregano
2 tbsp olive oil

Put the rabbit pieces in a bowl. Mix the marinade ingredients together in a bowl and use your hands to massage it into the rabbit pieces, making sure they are well covered. Season with salt and pepper and leave to marinate for at least a couple of hours.

Heat the olive oil in a heavy-based flameproof casserole over medium heat. Fry the rabbit pieces on all sides until evenly browned. Remove the rabbit from the casserole with a slotted spoon and add the onion. Sauté the onion until translucent and then add the chilli pastes. Cook for a further couple of minutes and then deglaze the base of the casserole with the white wine. Scrape vigorously to make sure nothing is sticking and then add the stock. Return the pieces of rabbit to the casserole. Cover and simmer over low heat for about 1 hour.

Meanwhile, boil the potatoes in plenty of water until they are firm but tender inside. Drain, and when cool enough to handle, cut the potatoes in half.

Stir the ground peanuts into the casserole and leave to simmer uncovered for a further 30 minutes until the sauce has thickened and the rabbit is very tender. Add the potatoes and leave them to heat through. Serve sprinkled with finely chopped parsley.

OUR FAVOURITE ANIMAL

Andean Peruvians love guinea pigs. They are bred with care, eaten as a delicacy and believed to be good luck charms even capable of curing diseases. *Picante de cuy* was one of my grandmother's favourites. She used to breed them in her mud-brick home nestled in the mountains. Her kitchen was quite basic and she kept her guinea pigs underneath the stove. They lived in great comfort in what was probably the warmest part of the house, but whenever there was a special occasion, her hand would reach into the guinea pigs' domain, looking for the fattest, best-fed specimen. This one would be used in her *picante de cuy*.

KIWICHA
S/ 6.60

QUIN
LAVAD

5
-
VEGETARIAN

THE SHEER VARIETY OF SOME OF PERU'S STAPLE CROPS IS MIND-BOGGLING.

I have always loved visiting the markets throughout Peru, not only for the spicy aromas of the different chillies, the coriander and cumin that always fill the air, but for the spectacle of the many multi-hued potatoes, beans, maize and quinoa that are ranged side-by-side. There are 2500 varieties of potato and 150 of sweet potato alone. Chillies, called ají, *come in different varieties; but some of the key ones, like* ají amarillo *and* panca, *are solely grown in Peru. The tomato is said to originate in Peru, as do over 650 different types of fruit, including the extraordinary* lúcuma *and* chirimoya *(custard apple). Maize comes from all over South and Central America, but in Peru we have purple maize as well as superfood cereals like quinoa,* kañiwa *and* kiwicha, *grown in the Andes. And in the Amazon we have fruits like* sauco *and* camu camu. *Some of the other edibles native to Peru also have great health benefits:* uña de gato *(cat's claw) is thought to help alleviate cancer and* yacon *helps diabetics.*

While you can treat most of the dishes in this chapter as side dishes, some of them, especially those containing beans, quinoa and pasta, are very hearty, complete meals, designed to sustain you through the day, and so they make perfect vegetarian main dishes. In Peru, vegetables are celebrated and are often the 'star' of any main meal. Their heritage is closely entwined with Mother Earth, so it's no wonder that there is an abundance of wonderful vegetarian dishes.

HUANCAINA MACARONI

MACARONI WITH HUANCAINA & CHEESE SAUCE *Pasta has become a staple in Peru, thanks to its introduction at the hands of Italian immigrants. This version of the classic macaroni cheese is given a spicy Peruvian hit by the inclusion of Huancaina Sauce.*

SERVES 4

500g dried macaroni
½ portion of Huancaina Sauce
(see page 232)
50ml single cream
100g mature Cheddar cheese,
    coarsely grated
1 tbsp olive oil
Salt

Bring a large saucepan of water to the boil and add some salt. Pour in the macaroni and cook according to the packet instructions until *al dente*.

Meanwhile, preheat your grill to its highest setting.

Put the Huancaina Sauce in a saucepan with the cream. Heat very gently and do not let it boil as you don't want it to separate.

Drain the macaroni and tip it into the warm Huancaina Sauce. Mix well and then pour into a large casserole dish.

Sprinkle over the cheese and then drizzle with the olive oil. Place under the hot grill and cook for about 10 minutes or until the top is golden brown and bubbling.

QUINOTTO DEL VALLE SAGRADO

MUSHROOM QUINOTTO Quinotto *is like a quinoa risotto, but the method is a little different – the quinoa is cooked before being added to the remaining ingredients. Quinoa is much healthier than white rice and the addition of wine, cream and cheese makes it just as indulgent as the Italian counterpart.*

Rinse the quinoa thoroughly. Put it in a saucepan and cover it with the cold water and a pinch of salt. Set over medium heat and bring to the boil. Reduce the heat and simmer for 10 minutes until all the water has been absorbed.

Meanwhile, put the olive oil and butter in a wide, shallow saucepan. Melt over low heat and then add the onion and mushrooms and sauté until the onion is soft and translucent. Add the garlic and sauté for a further minute and then add the wine. Bring to the boil and then add the cream and season with a grating of nutmeg and some pepper.

Bring back to the boil and add the cooked quinoa. Lower the heat and allow the quinotto to continue cooking, stirring constantly, until it has the same thick texture of risotto. Add half the Parmesan, half the parsley and some salt if necessary.

Serve with the remaining Parmesan and parsley sprinkled over the top.

SERVES 4

250g quinoa
1 litre cold water
1 tbsp olive oil
30g butter
1 onion, finely chopped
125g mushrooms, finely sliced
3 garlic cloves, finely chopped
125ml white wine
125ml single cream
Grated nutmeg, to taste
50g Parmesan cheese, grated
4 tbsp finely chopped flat-leaf parsley
Salt and freshly ground black pepper

PAPAS A LA HUATIA CON UCHUCUTA

HERITAGE POTATOES WITH UCHUCUTA SAUCE *Typically this dish is made in a huatia, a type of traditional earthen oven dating back to the Inca Empire, often made in the ground from rocks and bricks. For this recipe, try and use a mixture of some of the more interesting varieties of potatoes that are becoming available, as this method of cooking really brings out their distinctive flavours.*

SERVES 4

750g new, waxy or ideally heritage
   potatoes
25g coriander
25g flat-leaf parsley
10g mint
10g tarragon
100g crushed salt
1 portion of Uchucuta Sauce
   (see page 234), to serve
Freshly ground black pepper

Preheat the oven to 150°C (gas mark 2).

If necessary, cut the potatoes so they are the size of small new potatoes. Wash them, don't drain too thoroughly and put them in a bowl.

Roughly chop all of the herbs and mix together with some black pepper. Put half of the herbs in the bottom of a large casserole dish. Pour the salt over the potatoes and turn them over, making sure the salt is sticking – the water should help with this. Put the potatoes in the casserole and cover with the remaining herbs.

Put the lid on the casserole and bake in the preheated oven for 2–2½ hours, turning the potatoes every so often. Remove the lid for the last 30 minutes of cooking time in order to let any steam escape. The potatoes should be dry, with a powdery crust of salt clinging to the skin.

Serve with a bowl of Uchucuta Sauce for dipping.

PACHAMANCA AND HUATIA COOKING

Andeans love the earth and, for them, using the *pachamanca* (cooking with earth) method is the purest way to cook. Stones are heated over a fire, meat, potatoes, tamales, vegetables and beans wrapped in leaves are placed on top and then a conical mound of earth is built up over it to keep the heat in. This makes a natural oven that gives the food an earthy flavour. A variation of this, usually used for potatoes, is a *huatia* oven, named after a character from Incan mythology who masqueraded as a traveller who only ate potatoes. In this case, an oven is built from stones or mud bricks. Rocks are placed inside, along with kindling, and when they are hot, the food is added. At this point the oven will be covered with earth and will eventually collapse, 'burying' the food, which can be left to cook gently for hours.

CAUCHE DE QUESO PICANTE

SPICED CHEESE & VEGETABLES *This is a lovely dish found mostly in the south of Peru. Our variation works very well served family-style at the table, especially with lots of bread for mopping up on the side. Bake it in an oven-to-table earthenware dish or cast-iron casserole.*

SERVES 4

2 red onions, thinly sliced

4 tomatoes, peeled, deseeded and chopped

1 tbsp finely chopped flat-leaf parsley

1 tbsp finely chopped oregano

½ amarillo chilli, deseeded
    and finely chopped

1 tbsp olive oil

500g Paria cheese or haloumi,
    cut into thick slices

75ml single cream

2 tbsp water

Salt and freshly ground black pepper

Preheat the oven to 160°C (gas mark 3).

Mix the red onions, tomatoes, parsley, oregano and chilli together in a bowl and season well.

Drizzle some olive oil over the base of a casserole dish. Add a layer of the onion and tomato mix and then add a layer of the cheese slices. Repeat these layers until it has all been used up.

Mix the cream with the water and pour this over the contents of the casserole. Season with salt and pepper, cover with a lid and bake in the preheated oven for 30–40 minutes.

Serve in shallow dishes with some steamed new potatoes or some crusty bread.

NOTE
♦ Paria cheese is from the southern region of Puno in Peru. It's a semi-hard cows' milk cheese that can be tricky to find so we've suggested haloumi as an alternative.

CHUPE DE PALLERES VERDES

BROAD BEAN SOUP *This is a very restorative soup. The secret is in the vegetable stock, which should provide an incredible depth of flavour if made from scratch (see page 237). If you are using young broad beans, you do not need to remove their grey casing, but the colour of the finished soup will be better if you do.*

To make the soup, put the stock into a saucepan over medium heat and bring to the boil. Add the broad beans, celery, leek and half of the spring onions and simmer for 30 minutes or until tender.

Add the cooked rice and simmer for a further 20 minutes. Season well with salt and freshly ground black pepper and serve in bowls with the Parmesan and the remaining spring onions to garnish.

VARIATIONS

♦ You can of course vary what you put in the stock. Any non-starchy vegetable peelings are good if they are clean and unblemished.

♦ Try adding mushroom trimmings for an extra kick of savoury flavour, or some pumpkin or squash for sweetness.

♦ And if you really can't resist adding some meat, a ham hock bone pairs brilliantly with broad beans.

SERVES 4

2 litres Vegetable Stock (see page 237) or good-quality shop-bought vegetable stock
500g fresh broad beans, blanched and peeled
1 celery stick, finely chopped
1 leek, finely chopped
4 spring onions, trimmed and finely sliced
120g cooked white rice
50g Parmesan cheese, grated
Salt and freshly ground black pepper

TACU TACU DE PALTA

AVOCADO & RICE FRITTERS *A traditional and much-loved Afro-Peruvian dish usually made with leftover rice and beans, but here I have created a new version. The dish can resemble a hash brown, although it is cooked with rice rather than potato. Our version is made with avocado, which gives it a lovely, silky richness.*

Heat the olive oil in a frying pan over medium heat and sauté the onion for 10–15 minutes or until it is soft and translucent. Add the garlic and chilli paste and cook for another minute. Add the avocado and then transfer to a bowl with the rice. Combine thoroughly and season with salt and freshly ground black pepper. Transfer to the fridge to chill for 2–3 hours.

When the mixture is firm and cold, remove from the fridge and divide roughly into 4 equal portions. Dust each portion with a little flour.

Heat some vegetable oil in a non-stick frying pan set over medium heat. Using a spoon, heap a portion of the mixture into the pan and press down evenly with a spatula to form a rough oval shape. Try to fit 3 or more in your pan or cook in batches if necessary. Cook for 3–4 minutes until the bottom is a light golden brown. Turn each portion over and continue to cook until the fritters are a rich golden brown on both sides. Keep warm while you cook the other portions if you are cooking in batches, adding a little more oil as necessary.

Serve with some fried banana, some extra chopped avocado and a fried egg on top.

SERVES 4

1 tbsp olive oil

1 large onion, finely chopped

3 garlic cloves, crushed

1 tsp Amarillo Chilli Paste (see page 226)

1 large avocado, peeled, stoned
   and finely diced, plus extra to serve

Peruvian Rice (see page 136),
   made with 350g rice

Flour, for dusting

Vegetable oil, for frying

Salt and freshly ground black pepper

TO SERVE

4 bananas, peeled, sliced and fried

4 fried eggs

TACACHO

PLANTAIN BALLS *A favourite breakfast snack in the Amazonian region of Peru, they're usually cooked in pork fat and eaten with grilled gammon alongside a cup of strong black coffee. They also make a perfect side dish or starter served with a bowl of Amarillo Chilli Sauce (see page 232) for dipping.*

MAKES ABOUT 24 BALLS

Juice of ½ a lime
2 green plantains, peeled
   and cut into chunks
Oil, for frying
1 small onion, finely chopped
2 garlic cloves, crushed
10g coriander leaves, finely chopped
100g roasted peanuts, ground
Salt

Bring a large saucepan of water to the boil and add some salt and the lime juice. Add the plantains and simmer for at least 30 minutes until soft.

Heat some oil in a frying pan over medium heat and fry the onion and garlic for 15–20 minutes or until caramelised. Add the coriander and peanuts and stir through.

Drain the plantains and then transfer to a bowl. Using a fork, mash the plantains and then add the remaining ingredients from the pan and mix well.

Use your hands to shape the mixture into balls about 5cm in diameter. Flatten them slightly and place back in the pan with a dash of oil. Slow fry, for 3–4 minutes on each side, turning them until golden brown and slightly crispy. These tasty bites are also delicious served with a fried egg, grilled chorizo or bacon.

PEPIÁN DE PALLARES

BUTTER BEAN PURÉE *This is a very savoury butter bean purée that is perfect served with rice or as a side dish. It makes a good alternative to mashed potatoes as it's creamier and richer in taste. The traditional* pepián *uses meat and choclo instead of butter beans, but our chefs have created this innovative new version.*

SERVES 4

3 tbsp olive oil
1 large onion, finely chopped
1 amarillo chilli, finely chopped
3 garlic cloves, finely chopped
1 tsp smoked paprika
200g dried butter beans,
    soaked overnight in plenty of water
1 litre water
20g butter
Salt and freshly ground black pepper

Heat the olive oil in a large saucepan over medium heat and add the onion and chilli. Sauté for a few minutes until the onion has softened and is translucent. Add the garlic and sauté for another minute and then stir in the paprika. Add the soaked butter beans and pour over the water. Do not season at this stage otherwise the beans will toughen.

Bring the beans to the boil and spoon off any scum or foam that collects on the surface of the water. Reduce the heat and simmer the beans until they are cooked through and have started to disintegrate. This should take about 45 minutes, but could be longer, depending on how fresh the dried beans are. Keep an eye on the beans during the cooking process as you may need to add more water.

When the beans are very tender, beat in the salt and pepper with a spoon – the beans should easily break up and form a purée. Add the butter, stir and cook until heated through.

CAMOTE ANARANJADO

ORANGE-GLAZED SWEET POTATOES *We love this method of cooking sweet potatoes and these go well with so many Peruvian dishes, including some of our ceviches. You can change the recipe a little by using clementines instead of oranges and varying the spices according to taste.*

Preheat the oven to 150°C (gas mark 2).

Bake the sweet potatoes in their skins directly on the oven shelf for about 1 hour until they are cooked.

Peel and slice the sweet potatoes into 2cm slices; try to do this as cleanly as possible.

Put all the ingredients for the glaze in a saucepan. Simmer over low heat, stirring constantly, until the sugar has completely dissolved and then bring to the boil. Reduce the liquid until it is quite syrupy and then strain to remove and discard the spices.

Add the sweet potatoes to the syrup and gently turn them over until warmed through and covered in the glaze.

SERVES 4

2 medium sweet potatoes

FOR THE GLAZE
A pinch of salt
200g sugar
Zest and juice of 1 orange
3 cloves
1 star anise
5cm cinnamon stick
50g butter
200ml water

PASTEL DE CHOCLO

BAKED CORN CAKES *Edith Schneider is a wonderful Peruvian cook and a good friend of ours. I first ate this dish at her home and was so bowled over by it, I persuaded her to let me put it on the menu. It has become one of the most popular vegetarian dishes we serve.*

SERVES 4

500g choclo kernels (see page 223),
  corn-on-the-cob kernels
  or tinned sweetcorn
½ tsp salt
2 large eggs
65g butter, softened
1 tsp cornflour
1½ tbsp baking powder
1 tbsp granulated sugar
Olive oil, for greasing
100g Fresh Cheese (see page 239)
  or feta, cut into small cubes

Preheat the oven to 120°C (gas mark ½).

First cook the choclo kernels. Put them in a saucepan, cover generously with water and the salt and simmer over low heat for about 10 minutes until softened. Drain and set aside. If you are using tinned sweetcorn there is no need to cook it at this stage.

Separate the eggs. Put the yolks in a food processor or blender with the corn and blitz to a rough purée. Tip the blended mixture into a large bowl and stir in the butter, cornflour, baking powder and sugar. Mix thoroughly.

Whisk the egg whites until they're quite dry and have reached the stiff peak stage. Gently fold the egg whites into the rest of the mixture until completely incorporated keeping as much air in the mix as possible. A metal spoon is the best thing to use here.

Use some olive oil to grease a medium-sized casserole dish or a 20 x 20cm baking tin. Spread the corn batter over the base of the casserole dish or tin with a spatula or palette knife. Sprinkle over the cubes of cheese and push them into the mixture so they are almost completely covered by the batter. Place in the preheated oven and cook slowly for 2 hours. Remove the dish or tin from the oven, carefully empty out into a non-stick baking tray and return to the oven. Turn the temperature up to 150°C (gas mark 2) and cook for a further 40 minutes or until golden brown.

Remove from the oven and leave to cool a little before cutting into thick slices and serving.

VARIATION

♦ Although we prefer to bake this savoury vegetarian corn cake with added cheese, it is perhaps more common in Peru to use the corn mixture as a topping, often with a kind of Peruvian meat ragù. So if you'd like to give your shepherd's pie a bit of a Peruvian makeover, flavour up your sauce with a dash of cumin, some chillies, garlic and a few spoonfuls of tomato purée, add a few chopped raisins and olives and then cover with the corn cake batter. Then simply bake for about 1 hour in an oven preheated to 160°C (gas mark 3).

ARROCITO

PERUVIAN RICE *This is a very simple savoury rice that we use to accompany all kinds of dishes. It is also good with the addition of some choclo corn for some extra texture and taste.*

SERVES 4

2 tbsp vegetable oil
2 garlic cloves, crushed
200g long-grain rice
300ml water
½ tsp salt
Pinch of ground cumin

Heat the vegetable oil in a large saucepan over medium heat and add the crushed garlic. Sauté for a minute, making sure it doesn't start to brown, and then add the rice and cook for a further minute.

Add the water, salt and cumin, cover and bring to the boil. Turn the heat down to a simmer, cover and allow the rice to cook for 10–15 minutes or until all the liquid has been absorbed. Carefully stir the rice once with a fork to loosen it. Turn off the heat and leave to sit, covered, to steam for a few minutes.

ESPÁRRAGOS A LA PARRILLA

GRILLED ASPARAGUS *Peruvian asparagus is one of the best and most widely enjoyed in the world. This is a very simple way of cooking it. We always blanch the spears first so they don't dry out while they are being grilled.*

Cut the ends of the asparagus at the point at which they snap; this is where they turn from tender to woody, so discard the ends from there.

Bring a large saucepan of water to the boil over medium heat and add a pinch of salt, the sugar and the lime juice. Add the asparagus and parboil for 1 minute. Drain immediately and refresh under cold water. Drain thoroughly.

Put a griddle pan over high heat. When it is just smoking, arrange the asparagus spears over the griddle and brush with olive oil. Grill for about 4 minutes or until tender, turning regularly. Sprinkle with salt and pepper and a squeeze of lime. Serve with the Huancaina sauce.

SERVES 4

16 large asparagus spears
A generous pinch of sugar
A squeeze of lime juice
50ml extra virgin olive oil
1 portion of Huancaina Sauce
  (see page 232)
Salt and freshly ground black pepper

6

-

SALADS

IT'S HARDLY SURPRISING THAT PERU IS AND ALWAYS HAS BEEN AN AGRICULTURAL NATION. *The fertile terraces of the Andes, the dry coastal regions and the humid Amazonian rainforest have provided Peru with a bounty of foodstuffs. Some have been eaten for thousands of years and have become staples the world over (think of potatoes, maize and beans), some have only recently become popular outside of Peru and other Andean countries (quinoa) and some are just now being discovered. Chefs today are taking more interest in the lesser known ingredients that Peru's diverse regions have to offer, often showcasing them in ever-varied and interesting salads and vegetable dishes.*

We have kept some of the dishes in this chapter very simple on purpose, as these are dependent on the very best produce you can find. Eating seasonally will not only help you save cash; your dishes will taste all the better for it too. Dishes such as the Tomato and Red Onion Salad are best enjoyed if you are able to find tomatoes that are sweet and full of flavour. Quinoa, Butter Bean and Avocado Salad is a favourite of mine – the complexity of textures and flavours will make your mouth come alive. Other dishes, such as the Coriander Potato Cake with Beetroot and Avocado, show Ceviche chefs' creativity at its best. In Peru, there are endless varieties of causas *(potato cakes) – here we have included our favourite version and made it into a salad that has become one of the most-loved dishes at Ceviche. It's fresh, healthy and colourful, like all the best salads in the world.*

ENSALADA MIRAFLORES

CORN, BEAN & CHEESE SALAD *Butter or lima beans are used interchangeably with fresh or dried broad beans in Peruvian cuisine. If you would like a greener salad, use fresh broad beans here, blanching and peeling off their skins before adding to the remaining ingredients.*

SERVES 4

3 choclo cobs (see page 223)
   or corn-on-the-cobs
1 tbsp olive oil
100g smoked bacon lardons
1 x 200g tin of butter beans,
   drained and rinsed
1 large red onion, cut into 1cm dice
4 large tomatoes, deseeded and
   cut into 1cm dice
¼ of a rocoto, deseeded and very
   finely chopped
200g Fresh Cheese (see page 239)
   or feta, cut into small cubes
1 tbsp finely chopped flat-leaf parsley

FOR THE DRESSING
3 tbsp extra virgin olive oil
3 tbsp red wine vinegar
A pinch of sugar
A squeeze of lime juice
Salt and freshly ground black pepper

Bring a saucepan of water to the boil over medium heat and cook the choclo cobs until tender. Drain and plunge into iced water to cool down and then cut or break off the kernels from the cob.

Heat the olive oil in a frying pan over medium heat and sauté the bacon lardons for a few minutes until they are crisp and brown. Drain on kitchen paper.

Put the choclo or corn, butter beans, onion, tomatoes, chilli and cheese into a large bowl.

Whisk all the dressing ingredients together in a bowl or jug and pour into the bowl of salad. Gently toss everything together, trying not to break up the cheese.

Divide the salad between 4 shallow bowls and sprinkle over the bacon lardons and the finely chopped parsley.

ENSALADA DE HIGO Y QUESO FRESCO

SWEET FIG & FRESH CHEESE SALAD *This salad uses a mixture of cooked spiced green figs and fresh figs that should be at the peak of their ripeness. It is quite unusual in the way it combines sweet, salt, heat and spice – but it works!*

Put the green figs in a saucepan and add the spices, orange juice and sugar. Add water until it is just covering the figs and then heat over low heat, allowing the sugar to melt. When the liquid is syrupy and the figs are soft but still hold their shape, add the pisco. Remove from the heat and leave to cool down.

Cut the ripe figs lengthways into thin slices and arrange over 4 plates as you would for carpaccio, leaving a space in the middle of the plate. Remove the green figs from the syrup and lightly toss with the Fresh Cheese. Place this mixture in the centre of the plates.

Sprinkle over the limo chilli, basil and the shavings of Parmesan. Drizzle with a little olive oil and some of the syrup from the figs and serve immediately.

SERVES 4

12 green or fairly unripe figs,
    plus 8 ripe figs
5cm cinnamon stick
5 cloves
2 star anise
50ml orange juice
50g sugar
1½ tbsp pisco
100g Fresh Cheese (see page 239)
    or feta, cubed
1 limo chilli, deseeded and
    finely sliced lengthways
Some roughly torn basil leaves
    or micro basil leaves
20g Parmesan cheese, shaved
4 tbsp extra virgin olive oil

CAUSA SANTA ROSA

CORIANDER POTATO CAKE WITH BEETROOT & AVOCADO *A causa is a traditional layered dish made primarily of mashed potatoes. Our addition of beetroot, carrot and avocado makes a fun, psychedelic combination. They can be assembled in all kinds of moulds and you can vary the fillings as you like. It's a perfect vegetarian starter or light meal.*

SERVES 4

A handful of coriander sprigs
500g floury potatoes, unpeeled
A pinch of salt
1 tbsp Amarillo Chilli Paste (see page 226)
50ml vegetable oil, plus extra
    for deep-frying
50g sweet potato, sliced extremely fine
    lengthways
4 tbsp Olive Sauce (see page 234), to serve

FOR THE TOPPING

75g cooked carrots, diced
75g cooked beetroot, diced
1 limo chilli, finely chopped
1 tbsp finely chopped coriander leaves
3 tbsp mayonnaise
½ a small red onion, finely diced
1.5cm piece of ginger, peeled
    and finely chopped
Juice of ½ a lime
1 large ripe avocado, lightly mashed
Salt and freshly ground black pepper

First of all, prepare the potato. Put the coriander in a food processor or blender with a little water and blitz until it is puréed. Steam the potatoes with some salt until soft and, when cool enough to handle, peel and mash them. Add the salt and Amarillo Chilli Paste and then gradually add all of the oil, beating continuously, until the mash is smooth and coming away from the side of the bowl. Add the coriander purée to the mash and mix thoroughly. Be careful not to over mix or the mash will become chewy.

To make the topping: gently mix the carrots, beetroot, chilli, coriander, mayonnaise, onion, ginger and lime juice together in a bowl and then season with salt and pepper.

If you have a deep-fat fryer, heat the oil to 170°C. If not, pour the oil to a depth of about 5cm in a large, deep saucepan, making sure that it is no more than half full. To test if the oil is hot enough, drop in a cube of bread; if it sizzles and turns golden, the oil is ready.

Deep-fry the thin slices of sweet potato until crisp and until they start to take on a little colour – each one should look like a long, thin crisp. Take care not to burn them. With a slotted spoon, remove the sweet potato crisps from the oil and drain on some kitchen paper.

To assemble each *causa*, put an 8cm round mould on a plate. Put some mashed potato into it and press down to make a base layer. Top with a layer of mashed avocado and then a layer of the carrot and beetroot mixture. Remove the mould and serve with a few sweet potato crisps arranged on top Add a large spoonful of Olive Sauce on the side to serve.

ENSALADA DE QUINUA

QUINOA, BUTTER BEAN & AVOCADO SALAD *Quinoa is one of Peru's great superfoods. People love this Andean cereal and at Ceviche our customers are always asking for this salad recipe.*

SERVES 4

150g quinoa
100g butter beans, soaked overnight
   in water, drained and rinsed
25g coriander leaves, finely chopped
1 limo chilli, deseeded and finely chopped
1 ripe avocado, sliced very thinly
   on the diagonal
½ red onion, finely diced
1 large tomato, deseeded and finely diced
Salt and freshly ground black pepper

FOR THE PHYSALIS COULIS
10 physalis
1 tbsp granulated sugar

FOR THE DRESSING
Juice of 2 limes
1 limo chilli, deseeded and finely chopped
1 tbsp extra virgin olive oil

Wash the quinoa in cold water until it starts to run clear. Put in a saucepan, cover with cold water, add a pinch of salt and set over medium heat. Bring to the boil and simmer for 15–20 minutes until the quinoa is well cooked and the grain has started to unfurl. Drain, cool and set aside until needed.

Make the coulis. Put the physalis and sugar in a saucepan and add enough water to half cover the contents. Cook slowly over low heat until the water has reduced by two-thirds and the physalis are soft. Remove from the heat and leave to cool. Transfer to a food processor or blender and blitz until smooth.

Make the dressing. Put all the ingredients in a bowl and mix together well.

Add the butter beans, coriander and limo chilli to the quinoa and mix well. Add 3 tablespoons of the dressing, making sure you don't soak the quinoa mixture too much.

To assemble each salad, put a deep 10cm round mould on a plate (or use a large cookie cutter). Arrange a quarter of the avocado in the bottom of the mould and, using the back of a spoon, press down firmly. Fill the rest of the mould with the quinoa and butter bean mix and press down well again.

Pour a tablespoon of the physalis coulis around the mould and then remove it. Finally, mix together the onion and tomato and place a tablespoon of this on top. Add more dressing if you feel it's needed.

ENSALADA DE QUINUA CON UCHUCUTA

QUINOA SALAD WITH UCHUCUTA SAUCE *A fresh and multi-textured salad that has been given real bite by the addition of Uchucuta Sauce, or Andean hot sauce.*

SERVES 4

200g quinoa, washed in cold water
½ tsp of salt
2 garlic cloves, left whole and unpeeled
1 portion of Grilled Asparagus
    (see page 137), cut into 5cm lengths
1 large orange
100g Fresh Cheese (see page 239)
    or feta, crumbled
2 tbsp finely chopped coriander leaves
A small bunch of watercress
Freshly ground black pepper

FOR THE DRESSING

4 tbsp extra virgin olive oil
Zest and juice of 1 lime
2 tbsp Uchucuta Sauce (see page 234)

Put the quinoa in a saucepan and cover generously with cold water. Add half a teaspoon of salt. Pierce the whole and unpeeled garlic cloves with the tip of a knife and add to the saucepan. Set the pan over medium heat, bring to the boil and simmer for 15–20 minutes until cooked and the grain has started to unfurl. Drain and leave the quinoa to cool.

Put the cooled quinoa in a large bowl and add the grilled asparagus.

Next, segment the orange. Using a sharp knife, cut off the top and bottom of the orange, then cut the rest of the skin away – this is most easily done from top to bottom. Cut off any remaining pith, then holding the orange in your hand, cut the flesh along the membranes, as close as you can get. You should end up with membrane- and pith-free segments.

Squeeze the skin and remaining membrane over the quinoa and asparagus so as not to waste the juice, and add the orange segments to the bowl. Add the Fresh Cheese or feta and the coriander.

Make the dressing by whisking the olive oil, lime zest and juice and the Uchucuta Sauce together in a bowl. Pour this over the quinoa and asparagus and toss the whole thing together very gently. Season well with salt and freshly ground black pepper. Top the salad with sprigs of watercress to serve.

SOLTERÓN

PALM HEART SALAD *This is a good store cupboard recipe because it is best made using tinned palm hearts. Substitute small or waxy potatoes for the palm hearts for a very good potato salad.*

Put the sliced palm hearts, olives, chilli and Fresh Cheese or feta in a large bowl and mix together.

Mix the dressing ingredients together in a bowl or jug and pour over the salad ingredients. Toss gently. Check for seasoning and add salt and pepper if necessary.

Divide the spinach between serving plates and top with the dressed salad. Sprinkle with alfalfa sprouts to serve.

SERVES 4

200g tinned palm hearts, drained
   and cut into ½cm slices
80g pitted Peruvian botija olives
   (or use kalamata or any other
   black olive), chopped
1 amarillo chilli, finely diced
100g Fresh Cheese (see page 239)
   or feta, cut into 1cm cubes
50g baby leaf spinach
A small handful of alfalfa sprouts

FOR THE DRESSING
4 tbsp extra virgin olive oil
Juice of 1 lime
Salt and freshly ground black pepper

SOLTERITO TO SOLTERÓN

Located in the lower Andes is Peru's second largest city, Arequipa. It happens to be considered one of the many top gastronomic destinations in Peru. *Arequipeños* love eating out, particularly in open-air restaurants known as *picanterias*. One dish that usually features is a salad of broad beans, choclo and fresh cheese called *solterito*, literally meaning 'little bachelor'. At Ceviche we have taken the liberty of upgrading *solterito* to *solterón* by adding tasty ingredients, such as palm hearts and olives – still a bachelor, still fresh-faced, but a little more mature.

BRASILIA
VIVA
ERNESTO
Beto
PARDOS
EL QUE
VINO A
Y NO
PARA
CHICKEN
Chris
Nuestra
Comida
viva la comida peruana
Perú es grande
Solo mete
Sabor
Ritmo y Sabor
Cada plato tiene su historia
CAROL
MILI
INGENIERÍA
DEL PERÚ
MUNDO
USMP
COCINA
COME
le da
nuestra comida
DAS!
JB
LCBP

Wilberth Zuñiga
Presente
DESTRUCCION
DARWIN
ARACELY
TRIBUNA
ABIERTA
PINTAME
EVELYN
USMP
Jimmy
EL CHE PIERO
Zukhra was Here
JENNY REYNA
AV
DISCOVERY
Selene
JOAKIN
GLORIA
mueve
JESSICA
al Perú
Soy Peruano
Ritmo
GJ
LA COMIDA PERUANA ES
EL-FUTURO
Me INSPIRA
¡AMO MI COCINA PERUANA!
PASTELERIA NOVA
XIMENA
GASTON
CECILIA
Sabor

ENSALADA DE ALCACHOFA

ARTICHOKE HEART SALAD *If you find fresh artichokes during the summer, it is worth using them for this salad – or use artichoke hearts preserved in oil found at the deli counter. Avoid the tinned ones in brine as they won't taste as good.*

If you are using fresh artichokes, prepare them as follows. Fill a bowl with water and squeeze in a little lemon or lime juice. Cut the stalks off 5cm or so from the base, and peel off the tough green leaves until you reach the softer yellow ones. Cut the tips off these and peel the base. With a spoon, scrape out any furry choke and cut each prepared artichoke in half lengthways. Drop the hearts into the bowl of water as you go to stop them discolouring.

Place the prepared artichokes in a large saucepan of salted, boiling water and simmer for 10–15 minutes. Drain and leave to cool.

Make the dressing. Whisk the lime juice and olive oil (you could use some oil from the artichoke hearts if using ready-prepared) together in a bowl and add all the other ingredients. Leave to infuse for 30 minutes and then strain. Season with salt and freshly ground black pepper.

Cut the artichoke hearts (either the freshly prepared or the hearts in oil) into quarters and put in a bowl. Pour over the dressing and mix. Leave to marinate for 5 minutes.

Soak the red onion in iced water for 5 minutes and then drain and dry thoroughly with kitchen paper. Arrange the salad leaves over 4 plates and place the artichokes on top. Sprinkle over the red onion and chilli, drizzle over any remaining dressing and garnish with the torn coriander leaves or micro coriander.

SERVES 4

12 large artichokes, or 12 artichoke
   hearts in oil
A squeeze of lemon or lime juice
½ a red onion, finely chopped
A handful of lamb's lettuce
   or little gem leaves
1 limo chilli, very finely chopped
A few roughly torn coriander leaves
   or micro coriander

FOR THE DRESSING
Juice of 2 limes
4 tbsp olive oil
½ tsp coriander seeds, lightly crushed
½ tsp mustard seeds, lightly crushed
2cm piece of fresh ginger,
   peeled and sliced
2 garlic cloves, crushed
¼ of a rocoto, diced
Salt and freshly ground black pepper

ENSALADA DE TOMATE Y CEBOLLA

TOMATO & RED ONION SALAD *My great-aunts made this salad almost every day. They said that the vitamin A in the tomatoes would help me see in the dark and that the vitamin C in them would make me strong. But they were more obsessive about onions, which they swore cured any cold. I loved this salad and so did my other cousins, who would ask for this dish as soon as they walked through the door. None of us ever had colds as kids, but we couldn't see in the dark either.*

SERVES 4

1 large red onion, thinly sliced
1 tbsp extra virgin olive oil
Juice of up to 3 limes
400g perfectly ripe, sweetest tomatoes,
    preferably a mixture of varieties
    and colours
3 coriander sprigs, leaves finely chopped
3 flat-leaf parsley sprigs,
    leaves finely chopped
Salt and freshly ground black pepper

Soak the red onion slices in iced water for 10 minutes. Drain, dry and put these in a bowl.

Whisk the olive oil with the lime juice in a bowl, season with salt and black pepper and pour this over the onions.

Cut the tomatoes in half or wedges, depending on their size, and add them to the onions. Sprinkle over the coriander and parsley. Leave to sit for a couple of minutes and serve at room temperature.

PICA EL PEPINO

CUCUMBER & LIMO CHILLI SALAD *The contrast between the cooling cucumber and the tiny bit of heat from the chilli works very well in this simple salad.*

SERVES 4

4 tbsp granulated sugar
4 tbsp boiling hot water
1 medium cucumber, peeled
    and thinly sliced into rounds
1 limo chilli, finely chopped
4 tbsp white wine vinegar
Salt

Put the sugar in a cup and add the boiling water. Stir to dissolve the sugar and leave to cool in the fridge.

Place the cucumber in a bowl. In a separate bowl, mix all the other ingredients together including the cooled sugary water from the cup.

Pour the chilled sugar water over the cucumber, season with salt, cover and leave to marinate overnight in the fridge. Serve well chilled.

TIRADITO DE COLIFLOR

CAULIFLOWER TIRADITO *A very easy yet delicious salad where cauliflower is sliced very thinly. If you want a more rustic feel, leave the cauliflower in florets and simply toss it with the dressing.*

Bring a large saucepan of salted water to the boil over medium heat. Drop in the cauliflower and blanch for 1 minute. Drain and plunge into iced water to refresh it – you want the cauliflower to be on the crisp side.

To make the dressing, put all the ingredients in a food processor or blender and blitz until smooth. Strain the mixture through a sieve if you want it completely smooth.

To serve, cut the cauliflower florets into thin slices from top to bottom so you can lay them flat. Arrange over 4 plates and sprinkle the diced tomatoes on top. Drizzle over the dressing and serve immediately.

SERVES 4

1 medium cauliflower, broken into florets
4 medium tomatoes, deseeded
   and finely diced

FOR THE DRESSING
4 tbsp finely grated Parmesan cheese
3 tbsp extra virgin olive oil
3 tbsp white wine vinegar
1 tsp dark soy sauce
1 tbsp lime juice
2 garlic cloves, crushed

CEVICHE DE MANGO

MANGO CEVICHE *It may sound like an unusual combination – mango, onion and lime – but the flavours and textures in this ceviche really work. It is one of my favourite summer salads and is best made when mangoes are perfectly ripe.*

Put the red onion in iced water for 10 minutes while you prepare the other ingredients.

Place the diced mangoes into a bowl and add half the lime juice and salt. Taste for balance and add more of both if necessary; you don't want it to taste too sour. Add the chopped chilli, then drain the onion and add it along with the coriander leaves.

Stir everything gently to combine and then leave in the fridge for 5 minutes to chill and marinate.

Serve in individual large glasses or bowls.

SERVES 4

1 large red onion, thinly sliced
2 large ripe mangoes, peeled
   and cut into 2cm dice
Juice of 4 limes
¼ tsp salt
1 limo chilli, deseeded and finely chopped
2 coriander sprigs, leaves finely chopped

7
DESSERTS

MOST PERUVIANS HAVE A VERY SWEET TOOTH, AND I AM NO EXCEPTION.

We make sure desserts, cakes and biscuits are always the star of every celebration. Many of these tie in with religious holidays, such as the Sticky Anise Cake made every October for the Lord of the Miracles festival, or the Caramel Shortbreads eaten at Christmas time.

Before the Spanish conquistadors arrived the Incas enjoyed sweet dishes using sweet potato. They would leave it to dry out in the sun for several days, allowing the sugars to concentrate before caramelising on a barbecue. They would also make warm puddings from maize, corn and quinoa. Many Peruvian desserts either originate from or are heavily influenced by European originals. After all, the conquistadors introduced sugar cane, which probably kick-started the national fascination with desserts.

These origins, though, are only the start of the story. Afro-Peruvians improvised with less expensive molasses in their puddings. Staples such as black beans and corn were found to work well as desserts when cooked with sugars and spice. Also, of course, there is an abundance of fruit. Citrus fruits and other orchard fruits such as quince, brought over by the Spanish, are commonly used. While Peruvian elderberries and tropical fruits such as pineapple, passion fruit and the native physalis or goldenberry ensure that there is plenty of choice for anyone preferring tarter flavours. Finally, some fruits are almost desserts in their own right. Try the creamy chirimoya *(called 'custard apple' for a very good reason) or the* lúcuma, *which has a kind of maple syrup flavour. We use the* lúcuma *to make a wonderful ice cream that has become a favourite at Ceviche.*

SUSPIRO DE LIMEÑA

SPICED CARAMEL WITH PORT MERINGUE PUDDING *This Moorish-influenced creation of Italian meringue and Peruvian dulce de leche (*manjar blanco*) has existed in Peru since the early 1800s. When Amparo Ayarez created it for her husband (the poet José Gálvez), he renamed it* Suspiro de Limeña *in her honour as it is intensely sweet yet delicate, just like a 'Limenian woman's sigh'.*

SERVES 4

1 portion of Peruvian Dulce de Leche
(see page 241)
2 egg yolks
120g caster sugar
55ml white port
2 egg whites
1 tsp ground cinnamon,
plus extra for sprinkling
A few mint sprigs

First, make the Peruvian Dulce de Leche following the instructions on page 241. While that is still warm, whisk in the egg yolks and then heat gently to thicken. Strain the mixture into 4 dessert bowls or glasses and then chill in the fridge until needed.

Put the sugar and port in a small saucepan. Heat gradually, stirring until the sugar has dissolved and then bring to a fierce, rolling boil. You need this to reach the soft-ball stage, which is around 112–115°C. To test it has reached soft-ball stage, drop a small spoonful of syrup into a bowl of cold water. The syrup will form into a small ball, indicating it is done.

Meanwhile, whisk the egg whites briskly until they look opaque and form soft peaks. Pour in all the port syrup while it is still very hot and add the ground cinnamon. Keep whisking until the meringue is stiff and glossy – you will have made a soft, Italian-style meringue.

Spoon the meringue over the chilled Peruvian Dulce de Leche mixture and then decorate with a sprinkling of cinnamon and some mint.

VARIATION

♦ *Suspiro de Chirimoya* (Custard Apple Meringue Pudding): Peel, core and deseed 200g *chirimoya* (custard apple) and then mash it with a fork to purée. Mix the purée with half a portion of Peruvian Dulce de Leche (see page 241). Make the meringue, substituting the port for water in the sugar syrup, and then assemble the dessert as above.

AFROZ

SPICED RICE PUDDING *Rice pudding was introduced to Peru via the Spanish. Afro-Peruvians adapted it, using molasses instead of white sugar, so Afroz could be seen as rice pudding's more sophisticated sibling.*

Put the pudding rice in a medium-sized saucepan and cover with the water. Add the cinnamon sticks and cloves. Set over medium heat, bring to the boil and simmer until the rice is cooked and most of the water has been absorbed – this should take 25–30 minutes. Add the raisins for the last 5 minutes to help them plump up. You may need to stir occasionally at this point to make sure the rice isn't sticking.

Add the sugar and mixed spice, reduce the heat to low and cook for about 5 minutes, stirring regularly. Add the milk and cook for about 10 minutes, stirring regularly, until your rice pudding is thick and a rich golden brown. Remove the cloves and cinnamon sticks and serve in small bowls, sprinkled with the pecans and the coconut.

VARIATION

♦ For a slightly more grown-up version, you can infuse the raisins with pisco. Put the raisins in a saucepan, just cover with pisco and bring to the boil. Remove from the heat and leave to absorb for about 30 minutes before adding the raisins and a spoonful of the soaking liquid to the rice.

SERVES 4

200g pudding rice
800ml water
2 x 5cm cinnamon sticks
4 cloves
20g raisins
100g dark soft brown sugar
1 tsp mixed spice
400ml evaporated milk
20g pecans, roughly crumbled
2 tsp dessicated coconut

FREJOL COLADO

SWEET BLACK BEAN PUDDING *A popular dessert with children as the nutrition from black beans is cleverly hidden among the sugar and spices. It is best to purée the cooked beans with a hand-held blender to avoid having to add extra liquid.*

SERVES 4

150g black beans, soaked overnight
  in plenty of water
300g light soft brown sugar
2 x 5cm cinnamon sticks
3 cloves
A pinch of salt
75ml evaporated milk
2 tbsp sesame seeds

Put the beans in a large saucepan and cover with cold water. Set over medium heat, bring to the boil, skim off any foam that collects on the surface and simmer until cooked through and soft. Drain and then use a hand-held blender to purée the beans until they are as smooth as possible.

Put the puréed beans in a saucepan with the sugar, cinnamon sticks, cloves, salt and milk. Set over medium heat and stir carefully for 10–15 minutes while the sugar dissolves. Keep stirring for a few more minutes or until the mixture has thickened and you can see the bottom of the saucepan when you drag your spoon through it.

Remove from the heat and take out the cinnamon sticks and cloves. Stir in half of the sesame seeds.

Serve in individual bowls with the rest of the sesame seeds sprinkled on top.

CHAMPÚS

QUINCE & PINEAPPLE PUDDING *This is probably one of the oldest desserts in this book, but one of the most exotic and comforting at the same time. It is similar to the classic* mazamorra morada, *a purple maize pudding, but is easier to make. The warm quince and pineapple make it a perfect winter dessert.*

Dissolve the cornmeal in 250ml of the water in a bowl or jug.

Put the rest of the water in a saucepan over medium heat and bring to the boil. Add the orange zest and juice, cinnamon stick, pineapple and quince. Simmer for about 10 minutes or until the fruit is tender then add the sugar and the cornmeal mixture. Stir thoroughly and bring the whole mixture back to the boil. Cook for a couple of minutes and then add the soursop or *chirimoya*.

Serve hot, sprinkled with ground cinnamon.

SERVES 4

250g fine polenta
1 litre water
Zest and juice of 1 orange
5cm cinnamon stick
¼ pineapple, peeled and finely diced
1 small quince, peeled and finely diced
250g caster sugar
½ soursop (guanabana) or *chirimoya* (custard apple), peeled, deseeded and cubed
Ground cinnamon, for sprinkling

CHOCOLATE Y CAFÉ ENAMORADOS

MACHU PICCHU CHOCOLATE COFFEE POTS *The terraces of the sacred Inca site of Machu Picchu are world famous, but in recent years the name has also become synonymous with the superb quality fair trade Arabica coffee and cocoa beans that are grown in the surrounding valleys. This recipe marries the two together.*

SERVES 4–8

300ml single cream
50g caster sugar
100g dark chocolate, broken into pieces
1 tbsp strong Peruvian espresso coffee
1 tsp vanilla extract
2 tsp pisco
4 egg yolks

Preheat the oven to 150°C (gas mark 2).

Put the cream and sugar in a saucepan over medium heat and warm together until the sugar has dissolved. Turn up the heat and when the mixture has almost come to the boil, remove from the heat and leave to cool down a little.

Add the chocolate and stir until it has completely melted and then add the coffee, vanilla extract and pisco. Whisk the egg yolks in, one at a time.

Strain the mixture into a jug and pour into 4 ramekin dishes or 8 espresso cups. Put them in a large roasting tin and pour enough hot water to come up to halfway up the side of the ramekin dishes. Bake in the preheated oven for 20–25 minutes until the pots have set to a wobble.

Serve these either just warm or chill for a couple of hours. Either way, you might consider serving them with a Caramel Shortbread (see page 175) or two.

ALFAJORES

CARAMEL SHORTBREAD *These delicious little shortbread biscuits came to Peru via the Moorish influence on the Spanish. Variations are found all over Latin America, but sandwiching them with Peruvian dulce de leche (*manjar blanco*) is the way it is done in Peru.*

Sift the flours into a large bowl and mix. In a separate bowl, beat the butter with the icing sugar, egg yolk and vanilla extract until pale and creamy. Add the sifted flours and mix until everything comes together into a smooth dough. Form into a ball, wrap in cling film and chill in the fridge for at least an hour.

Preheat the oven to 160°C (gas mark 3).

Flour a work surface and roll out half the dough until it is about 5mm thick. Using a 5cm cookie cutter, cut out rounds from the dough and transfer to a baking tray lined with baking parchment. Repeat with the remaining dough.

Bake in the preheated oven for about 20 minutes, until they are a very light golden brown around the edges. Transfer to a wire rack to cool.

Sandwich the biscuits with the Peruvian Dulce de Leche and dust with icing sugar.

MAKES ABOUT 24 BISCUITS

250g plain flour, plus extra for dusting
50g cornflour
175g unsalted butter, softened and cubed
50g icing sugar, plus extra for dusting
1 egg yolk
1 tbsp vanilla extract
½ portion of Peruvian Dulce de Leche (see page 241)

VOLADORES

LITTLE FUDGE BISCUITS *These little biscuits might look dainty, but the flavours of the rich chocolate fudge and the sharp-tasting, fruity physalis sauce really pack a punch. You can serve them as a dessert in individual portions, but they are delicate enough to work well as petit fours.*

MAKES ABOUT 30 BISCUITS

3 egg yolks
2 tsp pisco
15g unsalted butter, softened
100g plain flour, plus extra for dusting
1 tsp baking powder
A pinch of salt
1 portion of Physalis Coulis (see page 243)

FOR THE FUDGE

100ml evaporated milk
25g caster sugar
100g dark chocolate (at least 70 per cent cocoa solids), broken into bits
10g unsalted butter

Preheat the oven to 160°C (gas mark 3).

First, make the biscuits. Using a handheld beater, whip the egg yolks in a bowl until they are airy and lighter in colour. You should be able to form a thick ribbon when you trail your whisk through them. Gradually mix in the pisco and the butter while mixing and then add the flour, baking powder and salt. Add a sprinkling of water, if needed. Knead the dough until it is smooth.

Roll out the dough to 1–2mm thick on a lightly floured work surface. Using a 5cm cutter, cut into rounds and put on a baking tray lined with baking parchment. Prick the rounds all over with a fork to prevent them puffing. Bake in the oven for 10 minutes or until a light golden brown and then remove and leave to cool.

To make the fudge, gently heat the evaporated milk and sugar in a saucepan and warm through until the sugar has dissolved. Remove from the heat, leave to cool for a couple of minutes and then stir in the chocolate and butter. Continue to stir until completely melted and you have a very thick, smooth fudge. Do not refrigerate as this will firm the fudge up too much and it will be hard to spread.

To serve, create stacks of the biscuits by sandwiching three together with some fudge. Place two stacks on a plate, dust with icing sugar and spoon some Physalis Coulis alongside. Decorate with a few whole physalis if you wish.

PICARONES

PUMPKIN & SWEET POTATO DOUGHNUTS *Typically found on the street corners of Lima, a* picarón *translates as a cheeky, mischievous person and these certainly live up to that name. They're fun to make, a bit messy and require patience, especially while you try to master the knack of forming rings of dough.*

SERVES 4

5cm cinnamon stick

4 cloves

1 tbsp aniseed

4 tbsp caster sugar

200g pumpkin (peeled weight), peeled, deseeded and chopped into chunks

200g sweet potato (peeled weight), peeled and chopped into chunks

20g fresh yeast (or 1 tsp dried instant yeast)

2 tbsp warm water

½ tsp salt

200g plain flour

Vegetable oil, for deep-frying

FOR THE SYRUP

200g dark soft brown sugar or Indian jaggery

1 cinnamon stick

1 star anise

6 cloves

1 fig leaf (optional)

1 orange, peel only

1 pineapple, peel only

First make the dough. Tie the spices into a bouquet garni using a small square of muslin (the aniseed will be difficult to remove otherwise) and put it in a saucepan along with 2 tablespoons of the sugar, the chopped pumpkin and sweet potato. Cover with water, bring to the boil and simmer until the pumpkin and sweet potato are soft. Drain thoroughly (you want it as dry as possible) and remove the bouquet garni. Mash the cooked pumpkin and potato (or transfer to a food processor or blender and blitz until smooth) and put in a large mixing bowl.

Meanwhile, dissolve the yeast in the warm water along with the remaining sugar. Leave in a warm place for 15 minutes until the mixture has started to develop a frothy head.

Add the salt and flour to the mashed or puréed pumpkin and sweet potato and then add the yeast mixture. Beat together until you have a smooth, slightly sticky dough. This might take a while; you can use the dough hook on your stand mixer if you prefer. Cover the bowl with a clean, damp tea towel and leave to rest in a warm place for 1 hour or until it has doubled in size.

While the dough is proving, make the syrup. Put the brown sugar or jaggery, spices and fruit peel in a saucepan and add water to cover. Bring to the boil and simmer until it has reduced to a thick syrup. Strain into a small bowl.

Using wet hands, form rings of dough by moulding a ball about 5cm in diameter and making a hole in the middle with the handle end of a wooden spoon. Swivel the spoon handle round and round, anti-clockwise, so the doughnut spins around it and the hole gets bigger (to get the right kind of action, imagine the spoon is you and the doughnut is a hula hoop!). When the hole is wide enough (about 4cm), put it to one side while you make the rest.

If you have a deep-fat fryer, heat the oil to 180°C. If not, pour the oil to a depth of about 5cm in a large, deep saucepan, making sure that it is no more than half full (you will need the doughnuts to be completely submerged though). To test if the oil is hot enough, drop in a nugget of dough; if it sizzles and turns golden, the oil is ready.

Fry the doughnuts in small batches in the hot oil. Flip the doughnuts over once during the frying process – you should end up with dark golden brown, crisp doughnuts.

Remove the doughnuts from the oil and drain on kitchen paper. Serve drizzled with the warm syrup and put any remaining syrup in a small bowl for dipping.

PASTEL DE QUESO CON SAUCO

ELDERBERRY CHEESECAKE *If I was making this in Peru, I wouldn't need to cook the elderberries with sugar first, as Peruvian elderberries are sweet enough to eat raw, but elsewhere they are much tarter, so here we've suggested cooking them in a citrusy sugar syrup first.*

SERVES 8

150g digestive biscuits
1 tsp ground cinnamon
50g unsalted butter, melted
200g Elderberry Jelly (see page 242)
Whipped cream, to serve

FOR THE FILLING

½ tsp ground cinnamon
Zest and juice of 1 lemon
Zest and juice of ½ an orange
200g caster sugar
100g elderberries
600g cream cheese
3 eggs
1 tsp vanilla extract

Preheat the oven to 160°C (gas mark 3).

First make the base by blitzing the biscuits in a food processor or blender. Stir the biscuit crumbs and cinnamon into the melted butter in a bowl and then spoon this into a 20cm non-stick cake tin (preferably springform or with a loose bottom). Press down firmly and then bake in the preheated oven for 5 minutes. Remove and transfer to the fridge to chill.

Make the filling. Put the cinnamon, lemon and orange juice and 2 tablespoons of the caster sugar in a saucepan over medium heat. Heat until the sugar is reduced and continue to simmer until the liquid is syrupy. Add the elderberries and heat through until they start to break up into the syrup.

Beat the cream cheese in a bowl until smooth. Add the orange and lemon zests, remaining sugar, eggs and vanilla extract. Gently stir in the elderberries and the syrup so you get a good marbled effect. Pour this mixture over the biscuit base. Cover the base of the cake tin in two layers of foil, folding it up the sides to prevent any water from leaking into the cake.

Place the cake tin in a large, deep roasting tin and pour boiling water into the roasting tin until it reaches halfway up the side of the cake tin. Bake the cheesecake in the preheated oven for about 50 minutes. When it is ready the texture should be firm with a slight wobble in the centre. Leave to cool and then chill for a couple of hours – this will improve the texture of the cheesecake.

Gently heat the Elderberry Jelly in a saucepan until it is runny. Pour this over the cheesecake and return to the fridge to set for a few hours. Serve in slices with a spoonful of whipped cream.

FLAN DE NARANJA

SOUR ORANGE FLAN *Flan (or* crème caramel *as it is also known) is hugely popular in Peru thanks to the Spanish influence. There are numerous variations; the classic version is made with milk and cream, but it can also be made with orange and other citrus fruits such as clementines.*

Preheat the oven to 150°C (gas mark 2).

Arrange 8 small ramekin dishes in a roasting tin large enough to hold them all with space in between.

Make the caramel. Gently heat the citrus juice and sugar in a saucepan, stirring until the sugar has completely dissolved. Turn up the heat and allow the sugar to boil; keep a close watch and remove from the heat once it is a deep, rich brown. Divide the caramel between the ramekin dishes, swirling each one around so the base and the bottom third of the sides are well coated.

To make the custard, zest 2 of the oranges into a pan and then juice all of the fruit; you will need about 400ml liquid. Add the sugar and slowly heat, stirring constantly to dissolve the sugar. Leave to boil fiercely for a couple of minutes.

Lightly whisk the egg yolks and whole eggs in a bowl until they are smooth, but not aerated. Pour over the hot orange syrup in a constant stream, whisking all the time and then strain through a sieve into a jug.

Divide this mixture between the ramekin dishes. Pour freshly boiled water into the roasting tin so it reaches halfway up the sides of the ramekins. Bake in the preheated oven for about 30 minutes or until the custards have set to a wobble. Remove from the oven, leave to cool and then chill, preferably overnight.

Before serving, dip each ramekin into a shallow bowl of freshly boiled water to make sure that the caramel will be liquid and the flans will turn out properly. Turn the flans out onto serving plates and serve unadorned.

SERVES 8

FOR THE CARAMEL
Juice of 2 Seville oranges
    or the juice of 1 orange and 1 lime
100g caster sugar

FOR THE CUSTARD
6 Seville oranges or 4 oranges and 2 limes
300g caster sugar
12 egg yolks
2 eggs

ENCANELADO DE PISCO

CINNAMON PISCO SYRUP CAKE *This light, airy cake can also be considered good for you as the sponge contains no oil or butter and, despite being soaked in sugar syrup, it isn't too sweet.*

Preheat the oven to 180°C (gas mark 4) and line a 30 x 20cm traybake tin with baking parchment.

First make the cake. Whisk together the egg yolks and half the sugar in a bowl until they have increased in volume, are very pale and stiff enough to hold a ribbon trail. Keep whisking while you add the vanilla extract.

In a separate bowl, whisk the whites until they form soft peaks and then gradually incorporate the rest of the sugar until you have a stiff, glossy meringue mixture.

Very carefully, fold in the meringue to the egg yolk mixture and then stir in the flour. Try and make sure your mixture doesn't lose too much volume at this stage. Pour the cake mixture into the prepared tin and bake in the preheated oven for 30–35 minutes until firm and a light golden brown on top. To test if the cake is done, insert a skewer into the centre. It should come out clean. Remove the cake from the oven and allow to cool.

Meanwhile, make the syrup. Bring the water, sugar, ground cinnamon and cinnamon stick to the boil, stirring constantly until all the sugar has dissolved. Remove from the heat and add the pisco.

Pour the warm syrup over the cooled cake and then chill for 2 hours. Cut into individual slices and dust with cinnamon. Serve with the Peruvian Dulce de Leche or ice cream and garnish with physalis.

SERVES 6–8

5 eggs, separated
200g caster sugar
2 tsp vanilla extract
100g plain flour

FOR THE SYRUP
75ml water
150g granulated sugar
1 tsp ground cinnamon, plus extra
    for dusting
1 large cinnamon stick
75ml pisco

TO SERVE
Peruvian dulce de leche (see page 241)
    or ice cream
A small handful of physalis

TURRÓN DE DOÑA PEPA

STICKY ANISE CAKE *Although the method is easy it is also quite involved, but don't be intimidated because the proof is in the first bite! It really is worth making, as the flavour is wonderful and it's a spectacular centrepiece for any celebration.*

SERVES 6–8

1 tbsp aniseed
100ml boiling water
450g self-raising flour,
    plus extra for dusting
200g cold unsalted butter
½ tsp salt
5 egg yolks
50ml aniseed-flavoured liqueur
    (a pastis or ouzo)
2 tbsp sesame seeds, toasted and ground
A selection of brightly coloured
    sugar-based cake decorations
    (the brighter, the better), to decorate

FOR THE SYRUP

400ml dark soft brown sugar
400ml water
Zest and juice of 1 orange
2 x 5cm cinnamon sticks
6 cloves

Preheat the oven to 160°C (gas mark 3).

Put the aniseed in a cup and pour the boiling water over it. Leave in the fridge to cool and infuse. Strain, discarding the aniseed and reserving the infused water.

Rub together the flour, butter and salt in a bowl until it resembles fine breadcrumbs You can do this by pulsing in a food processor if you prefer. Add the egg yolks, liqueur and sesame seeds and then gradually add the aniseed-infused water until the dough holds together (you may not need to use all of this).

Roll the dough out on a floured work surface until it is 2cm thick and then cut into 2 equal-sized squares. Place these on a baking tray lined with baking parchment, well spaced out, and then bake in the preheated oven for 20–25 minutes until golden brown.

Meanwhile, make the syrup. Put the sugar, water, orange zest and juice and the spices in a large saucepan over medium heat and bring to the boil, stirring as the sugar dissolves. Keep boiling until you have a thick, reduced syrup and until the mixture has reached the soft-ball stage. Test by dropping some of the syrup into cold water – it should form little soft balls. Optionally, it's much easier to test whether it's ready with a thermometer – it needs to reach 112–114°C. Use a slotted spoon to scoop out the spices and leave the syrup to cool for about 5 minutes.

To assemble the cake, line a square cake tin with greaseproof paper. Put one baked square on the greaseproof paper and spoon some syrup over the top. Repeat a couple of times.

Place the second square on top and spoon more syrup over the top. If any syrup seeps out, keep spooning back onto the top and down the sides. When the sides are sticky, the greaseproof paper will stay in place and help stop the syrup from escaping.

Decorate with a mixture of brightly coloured cake decorations – allow yourself full rein here! Leave to cool, preferably overnight as the syrup will set a little and the cake will be surprisingly easy to cut. Serve in small squares.

LORD OF THE MIRACLES

For the many Catholic *Limeños*, October is the most significant month of devotion, when the largest number of believers in South America take part in the festival of the Lord of the Miracles. This stunning spectacle has a 24-hour long procession and has taken place every year since the 17th century. Faithful followers dress in purple and make their way through the streets of Lima, spreading incense smoke, chanting beautiful laments and singing hymns. Of course, food is central to this celebration. Women selling *picarones* (see pages 178–179) and *anticuchos* (see Chapter 2) can be found on every street corner, but there is one recipe that is truly representative of this festival; the *Turrón de Doña Pepa*. The cake is named after Josefa 'Pepa' Marmanillo – an African slave who was allegedly cured of paralysis by the Lord of Miracles. She thanked him by making him this sweetly spiced creation and Peruvians have followed suit and made this an annual custom ever since.

HELADOS

ICE CREAMS *To simplify, we start with this base recipe, which is a traditional vanilla custard. It is delicious enjoyed as it is, but if you feel like experimenting with some Peruvian flavours, you could try the variations below.*

MAKES ½ LITRE OF ICE CREAM

250ml full-fat milk
100g caster sugar
1 vanilla pod, split lengthways
   or 1 tsp vanilla extract
3 egg yolks
250ml double cream

Put the milk and half the sugar in a saucepan with the split vanilla pod. Stir over low heat until the sugar has dissolved and then allow the milk to almost come to the boil. Take off the heat and leave this mixture to infuse until it has cooled.

Meanwhile, put the egg yolks in a bowl with the rest of the sugar and whisk until the mixture has a thick, mousse-like consistency and falls in thick ribbons.

Reheat the milk over medium heat until it again almost comes to the boil and then pour over the whisked eggs and sugar. Stir to combine and then pour the mixture back into the saucepan. Stir over very gentle heat until it has thickened – it will be the right consistency when you can draw a line with your finger across the back of a coated wooden spoon. Leaving the vanilla pod in, chill the custard thoroughly.

When you are ready to churn your ice cream, combine the custard with the double cream and strain through a sieve. Pour the strained mixture into an ice cream machine and churn until thick and frozen. If you don't have an ice cream machine, freeze in a large, shallow container, whisking every 30 minutes until it is the right consistency.

Garnish with chocolate and caramel shards and fresh mint to finish if you like.

FLAVOUR VARIATIONS

♦ *Avocado Ice Cream*: Make the ice cream up to the point when you need to add the cream. Purée the flesh of 2 avocados with the juice of 2 limes in a food processor or blender and then stir this into the custard. Strain through a sieve and add the double cream. Taste, and add 3 tablespoons caster sugar if needed. Churn and freeze as for the main recipe.

♦ *Manjar Blanco Ice Cream*: Make the Peruvian Dulce de
   Leche as on page 241 – you will need half the quantity for
   this ice cream. Make the base ice cream, but replace the
   caster sugar with light soft brown sugar. When you have
   churned the ice cream and before it has frozen solid, stir
   the spiced caramel into it. You are after a marbled effect,
   not uniformity. Leave to freeze completely; you will find
   when you serve it that you will have lovely soft pockets
   of the caramel throughout the ice cream.

♦ *Lúcuma Ice Cream*: Use *lúcuma* pulp (see page 224) wherever
   possible, but if you can't get hold of it, use 1 packet of
   lúcuma powder (see Suppliers, page 246), around 70g, and
   pour over 70ml water. Stir thoroughly and leave to stand
   for 2–3 hours until you have a purée. Make the base ice
   cream as for the *Manjar Blanco* Ice Cream. Before you add
   the cream, stir in the *lúcuma* purée and then strain through
   a sieve. Stir in the cream and then churn and freeze as for
   the main recipe.

SORBETE DE AGUAYMANTO

PHYSALIS SORBET *The flavour of physalis is hard to pin down; it's slightly citrusy, slightly tropical and quite unique. I think it has just the right combination of sweet and tart notes, so it's perfect in this sorbet. For the best results, when choosing physalis (pictured right), try to find unblemished berries.*

SERVES 4

250g physalis
300ml Sugar Syrup (see page 241)
Juice of ½ a lime
1 egg white

Remove and discard the papery husks from the physalis and wash them thoroughly as they might be slightly sticky. Put them in a food processor or blender with the sugar syrup and the lime juice. Pulse several times until the fruit has completely broken down and combined with the liquids.

Strain the mixture through a fine sieve in order to remove the seeds. Return the mixture back into the food processor or blender and add the egg white. Pulse several times until the mixture is well-blended and looks fluffy. Transfer to the fridge to chill.

If you have an ice cream maker, use it to freeze and churn your sorbet. If not, put the mixture in a sturdy airtight container and freeze. After 1–1½ hours, whisk the sorbet again either with a fork or an electric hand whisk, incorporating as much air as possible. Put the lid back on and continue to freeze for a further hour. Take out of the freezer and stir again and then freeze for a further hour. Repeat this once more and freeze until frozen.

Remove the sorbet from the freezer around 30 minutes before you are ready to serve it and transfer to the fridge. This will let it soften so that it can be scooped out easily.

8

–

DRINKS

THIS CHAPTER CONTAINS A SELECTION OF CEVICHE'S FAVOURITE COCKTAILS.

Some are based on Peruvian classics made popular in the early 20th century in Lima; others date back to pre-Prohibition America. There are also new creations from our team. These cocktails have been inspired by many things, including our love of pisco and the Peruvian tradition of infusing it with some wonderful fruits and spices, but perhaps above all they are inspired by Ceviche's Soho surroundings. Our neighbourhood has an artistic and bohemian heritage and brims with originality. We wanted Ceviche to reflect this 'buzz' and nowhere is that more apparent than in our cocktails.

At the heart of any great Peruvian cocktail is pisco, a light and luxurious clear spirit, which is distilled pure from grapes. The exact origin of its name is not certain. The word 'pisco' comes from the Quechua dialect; 'pishco o pisko', meaning 'bird'. These are abundant in the coastal regions of Peru. Pisco is also the name of a coastal town in the Ica Valley founded in 1640, but before then, in the same area south of Lima, there lived an indigenous community named Piskos who were expert ceramicists. It is said that they created the pots that became known as **piskos,** *which in turn gave the spirit its name. What is a fact is that the town of Pisco became a major port where pisco and wine were shipped to Europe and where the spirit became popular with a large community of international sailors and travellers.*

Piscos vary enormously, depending on what type of grape is used and where the grapes are grown. 'Non-aromatic' or 'aromatic' grapes are used either singly or blended to give each pisco different characteristics. The spirit isn't aged in the same way as other spirits, just rested for at least 3 months in glass, stainless steel or anything else which will preserve rather than change its flavour. However, what piscos do have in common with other spirits is that many are distinctive enough to be enjoyed on their own, neat (a top-class artisan Italia), while others have a less aromatic and purer flavour more suited to cocktail making. The pisco we prefer to use in most of our cocktails and infusions is our own blend, Pisco Acholado.

THE EVOLUTION OF THE PISCO SOUR

Peru's famous national cocktail was invented by an American called Victor V. Morris. He hailed from Salt Lake City and moved to Lima in 1903 to work for a railway company, but eventually opened Morris' Bar. This is where he invented the Pisco Sour as an alternative to the trendy Whisky Sour. Morris' Bar attracted a distinguished and mainly English-speaking clientele, including diplomats and politicians as well as writers and artists, so it's hardly surprising that the popularity of the Pisco Sour spread beyond Lima and Peru. Morris' Bar closed its doors shortly before the death of its owner in 1929. An original, handwritten recipe for the Pisco Sour has never been found. However, some of the Morris' Bar bartenders decamped to established hotels in Lima such as the Bolivar, Crillón and Maury, and they took their knowledge of how to prepare the drink with them.

PISCO SOUR

The classic cocktail, and this is our way of doing it. As everyone's tastes for sugar and sour vary, it's definitely one you can play around with to suit yourself.

There are two ways to make this cocktail. You can either put all the ingredients into a blender with 3 ice cubes and blend until smooth, or you can fill a shaker with ice, add the other ingredients and shake vigorously for at least 30 seconds.

Carefully hold the froth back with the lid of the shaker or blender and pour the liquid into a chilled glass; you will still end up with a drink with a good head of foam. To serve, add 3 drops of bitters.

NOTES

♦ Chuncho bitters is a Peruvian bitters made from Andean herbs. It's easy to get hold of, but Angostura bitters makes an excellent substitute.

♦ If you need to make more than one drink, note that one egg white will make enough froth for 4 drinks if blended or 2 drinks if shaken.

VARIATIONS

♦ We make all kinds of infusions with our pisco and use these to make sours. The ones we serve most frequently at Ceviche are the Physalis (*Aguaymanto*) Sour and the Chicha Sour. You can make them in exactly the same way, just substitute the Pisco Acholado with one of the infusions on page 216.

♦ If you do decide to make the Chicha Sour, you should reduce the amount of egg white by half, as the pineapple skin in the infused pisco will create a foam when blended or shaken.

SERVES 1

50ml Pisco Acholado
1 egg white
3 drops of Angustura or chuncho bitters

FOR THE SOUR MIX

30ml lime juice
20ml sugar syrup (see page 241)

PISCO PUNCH

This vintage cocktail gained worldwide fame thanks to a mention in the literary works of Mark Twain and Rudyard Kipling.

First, make the pineapple syrup. Put the Sugar Syrup, cubed pineapple and juice in a saucepan and bring to the boil. Immediately remove from the heat and leave to cool down completely, giving it time to infuse. Strain into a sterilised jar (see page 227) and keep in the fridge until needed.

Measure out 20ml of the prepared pineapple syrup and put it in a shaker. Add the remaining ingredients and fill with ice. Shake vigorously and strain into a chilled margarita glass.

NOTE

♦ You can keep the leftover pineapple syrup in the fridge for at least a month. It's fantastic as a concentrate for cordial or drizzle it over coconut ice cream or pancakes.

SERVES 1

50ml pisco (preferably Pisco Acholado)
1 tbsp lime juice
2 drops of grapefruit bitters

FOR THE PINEAPPLE SYRUP
100ml Sugar Syrup (see page 241)
¼ pineapple, peeled, de-eyed and cubed
200ml pineapple juice

ALGARROBINA

The algarrobina *is a variety of black carob that is made into a treacle-like syrup, slightly bitter, with a smoky flavour. It's available in health food shops, but if you can't find it try date syrup or black treacle instead.*

Measure all the ingredients, except the cinnamon, into a blender. Add 4 ice cubes and pulse until smooth.

Pour into a hurricane glass or a bulbous wine glass and sprinkle with a pinch of cinnamon.

SERVES 1

35ml Pisco Acholado
15ml crème de cacao (chocolate liqueur)
50ml evaporated milk
15ml Sugar Syrup (see page 241)
15ml *algarrobina* (black carob) syrup
1 egg yolk
A pinch of ground cinnamon

MARIA SANGRIENTA

A unique take on a Bloody Mary, the Maria Sangrienta is perfect as an accompaniment to brunch. We also recommend drinking it after a hard night as the chilli and tiger's milk have a miraculous warming and energising effect.

SERVES 1

35ml Limo Chilli-infused Pisco
   (see page 216)
1 shot of Rocoto Tiger's Milk
   (see page 230)
½ tsp Amarillo Chilli Paste (see page 226)
125ml tomato juice

TO DECORATE

A crack of black pepper
1 celery stick

Fill a shaker with ice and add all the ingredients. Gently roll the shaker around, be careful not to shake it too vigorously otherwise the tomato juice will lose its colour.

Pour the contents, including most of the ice, into a highball tumbler and decorate with a crack of black pepper and a celery stick.

VARIATION

♦ To make a non-alcoholic version, replace the pisco with more tomato juice.

PASIÓN DE CEVICHE

Instead of using ginger-infused pisco you could add grated ginger (and any juice) to some warmed honey syrup. Leave it to infuse until cool and strain before using.

SERVES 1

35ml Ginger-infused Pisco (see page 217)
15ml Prickly Pear Liqueur
   or apricot brandy
25ml passion fruit pulp
15ml Honey Syrup (see page 241)
5ml pineapple juice
A pinch of ground cinnamon

Fill a cocktail shaker with ice. Add all the ingredients, except the cinnamon, and shake very hard for at least 30 seconds.

Strain into a well-chilled Martini glass; it should have a good head of foam to it. Dust with a pinch of ground cinnamon and serve immediately.

SOHO PISCO

A signature drink we created especially for our restaurant in Soho that has quickly become a Ceviche classic.

Put all the ingredients, except the pepper, into a cocktail shaker and fill with ice. Shake thoroughly and strain into a chilled margarita glass. Then add the black pepper on top.

SERVES 1

25ml Limo Chilli-infused Pisco
  (see page 216)
25ml Elderflower Liqueur (see page 243)
1 scant tbsp lime juice
1 sliced round of cucumber
1 egg white
A light sprinkling of cracked black pepper

TORO MATA

'Toro Mata' is a popular Afro-Peruvian song and is played at the many late-night venues (peñas) in Lima and surrounding towns. They serve food and drinks, offer lively music and dance events and inspired this Ceviche creation.

Put all the ingredients, except the coffee beans, in an ice-filled cocktail shaker. Shake thoroughly and strain into a well-chilled Martini glass – it should have some froth, but not too much. Decorate with the coffee beans.

SERVES 1

25ml Coffee-infused Pisco (see page 216)
25ml Pisco Acholado
1 shot of espresso
15ml Sugar Syrup (see page 241)
A few coffee beans, to decorate

SOFÍA DEL MAR PUNCH

Thanks to the magnificent waves of Peru's coastline, surfing culture is thriving, but few are as good at it as Peruvian and world champion Sofía Mulanovich, to whom this cocktail is dedicated. With beachside attitude, this is a new take on the Piña Colada – with added kick and flavour.

Fill a cocktail shaker with ice and pour in all the liquid ingredients, except the rum. Shake vigorously and pour into a hurricane glass, ice and all.

Carefully pour the rum over the back of a spoon into the glass; it should float on top. Dust with a pinch of allspice and decorate the side of the glass with a physalis.

SERVES 1

35ml Physalis-infused Pisco
  (see page 216)
15ml apricot brandy
25ml sweetened coconut milk
25ml pineapple juice
15ml lime juice
25ml dark rum

TO DECORATE
A pinch of ground allspice
1 physalis

CHILCANO

At Ceviche we love this drink, especially when it's made with Eucalyptus-infused Pisco (see page 217). It brings a whole new meaning to the word 'refreshing'.

SERVES 1

50ml Pisco Acholado
Juice of ½ a lime
Ginger ale, to top up
2 drops of Angostura bitters
Slices of lime

Pour the pisco and lime juice into a highball glass and fill the glass with ice cubes. Top up with ginger ale, add the bitters and drop in a couple of lime slices to serve.

EL CAPITÁN

This is our interpretation of a Manhattan. We've given it a bit of a twist with the addition of Cherry-infused Pisco, but you can use twice the volume of Pisco Acholado if you prefer.

SERVES 1

25ml Pisco Acholado
25ml Cherry-infused Pisco (see page 217), plus a cherry from the bottle to serve
25ml sweet vermouth (we use Martini Rosso)
A dash of creole bitters (Angostura will do)

Take a large mixing glass and fill it two-thirds full with ice. Pour in all the liquid ingredients except the bitters and stir with a spoon until it is very cold. Strain into a well-chilled Martini glass. Add a dash of bitters and serve with one of the infused cherries.

MAKAHA COOLER

This 'mocktail' recipe uses soursop (guanábana), which can be bought as a juice, but if you can get hold of the fresh fruit, it will be worth it. This cooler is silky smooth with a hint of citrus that balances perfectly with the pear and honey.

Fill a cocktail shaker with ice and add all the ingredients, except the nutmeg. Give it a short but firm shake. Fill a highball glass with ice cubes and pour over the liquid. Sprinkle with a pinch of finely grated nutmeg.

NOTE

♦ If you would prefer to make the pear purée rather than buy it, simply blend a very ripe peeled pear with 1 tablespoon caster sugar and 1 teaspoon of lime juice.

SERVES 1

25ml pear purée or juice
1 tbsp lime juice
1 tbsp Honey Syrup (see page 241)
125ml soursop (*guanábana*) juice
Grated nutmeg, to serve

SUPERCHACO

A zesty, colourful 'mocktail'. As befits a drink named after a superhero artist, we have included maca powder – a ground root, which is yet another of Peru's indigenous superfoods, available from all health food shops.

Put all the ingredients, except the lemongrass and soda water, into a cocktail shaker and top with ice. Shake just enough to make sure that the maca powder is properly dispersed. Pour into a highball glass with some of the ice and top up with soda water.

Cut the bottom end off the lemongrass stick and peel off the outer layer in one piece, letting it curl back in on itself. Repeat this with the second layer and combine the two together. You should end up with a hollow stick of lemongrass, which should work as a straw for an extra little hit of flavour.

SERVES 1

15ml lime juice
25ml ginger and lemongrass cordial
1 tsp maca powder
75ml guava juice
Soda water, to top up
1 lemongrass stick

CHICHA MORADA

This is a popular non-alcoholic drink in Peru, where it is valued as a refreshing health drink. The purple maize gives the drink a beautifully deep purple hue.

SERVES 4

1.5 litre water
1 cob of purple maize
The skin of ¼ of a pineapple
½ an eating apple, unpeeled and diced
½ a quince, unpeeled and diced
1 clove
2cm cinnamon stick
6 tbsp granulated sugar
Juice of 1 lime

Put all the ingredients, except the lime juice and sugar, in a pan. Bring to the boil and simmer over low heat for 30 minutes. Take the pan off the heat, stir in the sugar and leave to infuse until cool.

To serve, add the lime juice and pour over lots of ice. Add a couple of slices of lime if desired.

NOTE

♦ This will store very well as it is, just make sure that you don't add the lime juice until you are ready to drink it as it will turn bitter.

MACERADOS

VARIOUS PISCO INFUSIONS *Infusing pisco has always been a Peruvian tradition. At Ceviche we have created some entirely new infusions using British fruits, such as raspberries and figs, some typically Peruvian infusions using Amazonian fruits, such as camu camu and physalis and some using an array of chillies. An infusion can be as simple or as complicated as you like – it's such good fun to experiment! Try starting with Pisco Acholado as it will complement rather than overwhelm the other ingredients in your cocktail. Use the freshest and best-quality ingredients you can and avoid any blemished fruits as they will really impair the flavour. We've recommended various infusion times. After the minimum time given, you can strain your pisco and rebottle it, but in some cases you can leave it be. As a general rule, an infusion that uses soft fruit (raspberries and strawberries) benefits from straining, but an infusion using hard, woody spices, herbs and beans (coffee and cocoa) can be left unstrained.*

Here are some of our house favourites to get you going. All the recipes make 1 litre of infused pisco so the quantities can be easily halved. We recommend storing your infusions in a cool, dark place.

LIMO CHILLI

Add 5 whole limo chillies to 1 litre pisco. This is probably the quickest of all our infusions to make as you will get the best flavour after only 3 days. You can leave the chillies in the pisco after this period, but you will need to dilute it with more pisco as the chilli flavour will continue to intensify. At Ceviche, we love using Limo Chilli-infused Pisco in our version of the Bloody Mary and also in our popular Soho Pisco cocktail (see pages 206–207).

PHYSALIS

Remove the papery husks and the stems from 150g physalis. Score a cross into each one to help release the flavour and add to 1 litre pisco. Infuse for at least 1 month. Try replacing the non-infused pisco with this in our classic Pisco Sour cocktail (see page 201).

COFFEE

Add 2 shots of espresso, the same amount of sugar and 50g of roasted whole coffee beans to 1 litre pisco. This needs to infuse for at least 2 weeks, but preferably for a month or more, and there is no need to strain away the coffee beans at any point beyond this as the flavour will not be impaired.

CHERRY

Remove the stems from 150g sweet, ripe cherries and add them to 1 litre pisco along with 75g sugar. You can vary the amount of the sugar; if your cherries aren't particularly sweet, you could add slightly more. Make a small incision on each cherry to help release the flavour. You could also stone a few of the cherries and crush the kernels into the pisco as this will add a slight almondy note to your infusion. It improves with age, so infuse for at least 2 weeks or up to 2 months. The cherries in this infusion can easily be substituted with other stone fruits such as plums and apricots.

EUCALYPTUS

Make sure the eucalyptus you use is suitable for eating – some of them are grown for decoration and will have been sprayed. If you are using fresh leaves, use 8–10; if dried, add a couple more. Add them to 1 litre pisco and infuse for 1–2 weeks, the longer the better.

GINGER

Take 125g peeled root ginger and finely chop half the quantity then grate the rest, ensuring that all the juice is captured and added to 1 litre pisco. You can use this after 1 week, but it will be better after 2 weeks.

PURPLE MAIZE

Add 1 cob of purple maize, the skin of ¼ of a pineapple, ½ an unpeeled and diced eating apple, ½ an unpeeled and diced quince, 1 clove and a stick of cinnamon to 1 litre pisco and to leave to macerate for at least 2 weeks before you start using it. The colour will turn a deep purple after 2 days.

9

—

THE PERUVIAN LARDER

THIS SECTION INCLUDES AN OVERVIEW OF PERUVIAN INGREDIENTS AND SOME BASIC RECIPES TO HELP YOU ON YOUR JOURNEY THROUGH PERUVIAN CUISINE.

Peruvian food is undoubtedly incredibly varied. There are very good reasons for this. First of all, there is the country itself. It is a place of extremes, with over 80 microclimates, and biodiversity across its three main terrains: the hot and dry coastal regions where citrus fruits thrive; the plateaus and terraces of the Andean Mountains that provide cool, high-altitude conditions perfect for potatoes, beans and quinoa; and finally the humid rainforests of the Amazonian basin, which provide much, but are still largely untapped. All of these factors means there is a lot of choice in interesting ingredients that bring a whole host of new flavours.

The rich culinary cultures of cities such as Cuzco and Arequipa, along with Lima, are constantly evolving. This variety, depth and modernity is helping Peruvian food gain popularity all over the world. While it is impossible to find the same variety of foods outside of Peru, things are gradually improving and becoming more readily available elsewhere. Take, for example, the increase in varieties of Peruvian potatoes or superfoods that are finding their way onto the shelves of our healthfood shops and local supermarkets. Hopefully this will continue on so we can enjoy more of this delightful cuisine.

The selection of basic recipes in this chapter act as building blocks for some of the other dishes in the book. Some are indispensable, such as Salsa Criolla (see page 236), which you will find is used frequently as a garnish, and some will be a useful addition to your Peruvian repertoire. Some recipes in this chapter are less necessary as the pre-prepared ingredients are available to buy; Fresh Cheese (Queso Fresco) and Huachana Sausage can be subsituted with feta cheese and chorizo sausage when they crop up in recipes, but if you are feeling adventurous, do try to make them at home as the end result will be even more rewarding.

VEGETABLES

The most popular vegetables in Peru are easily available elsewhere in the world; onions, root vegetables and cauliflowers, as well as spinach and chard, are eaten all year round. Peru also has the perfect growing conditions for ingredients such as asparagus and peas.

POTATOES

If you ever visit Peru you will be amazed by the number of different kinds of potato available, in a variety of beautiful colours, including red, yellow, orange and blue – a colour not often associated with food. Potatoes flourish – in the high altitudes of the Andes but also travel well and are exported around the globe. We will never have quite the same variety in the UK, but more are becoming available.

Whenever you get the chance, try experimenting with some different varieties, particularly in our Potatoes with Uchucuta Sauce recipe (see page 120), as you will be surprised by the subtle differences in flavour and textures. Not only are potatoes enjoyed freshly cooked they are also popular dried. This method of preserving potatoes is centuries old and ensures getting the most out of one humble ingredient.

CASSAVA

A brown, rough or hairy-skinned tuber, which is treated much the same way as potato, so it's usually boiled, mashed or fried. We use it to make fried wedges and mash it for our croquette balls (see page 46).

SWEET POTATO

There are over 150 types of sweet potato in Peru with varying skin and flesh tones as well as degrees of sweetness; some are much nuttier in flavour. The best way to cook them is to bake them whole in the oven as you would a potato, although they also make very good chips.

MACA

A Peruvian ingredient that has been hailed as a superfood. Maca is a root with an odd appearance with varying degrees of sweetness that grows well in the harsh, cold conditions in the Andes. It is prized because it's so good for you, with a balance of carbohydrates, proteins and oils, as well as a host of vitamins and minerals. Peruvians love it for its medicinal properties – it is often regarded as an aphrodisiac. Here in the UK maca is available in powder form and can be added to drinks or sprinkled over cereals and desserts. We use it in one of our non-alcoholic cocktails, called Superchaco (see page 211).

PLANTAIN

Arguably, this is strictly a fruit because it is a member of the banana family, but its starchy texture means it is often treated like a vegetable. It can be eaten ripe or green, but should always be cooked. If you are peeling a batch of them, drop the pieces into a bowl of cold water with a squeeze of lemon to stop them turning black. It is so versatile, you can also mash it into cakes or balls and fry it as chips or crisps (see page 52).

We mainly add it to salads, but it also has other uses; it's a healthy alternative to rice so we use it in Quinoa and Ceviche Rolls (see page 32), in Mushroom Quinotto (see page 119) and even as a crunchy coating for anything you want to deep-fry. Different varieties of quinoa that are multicoloured are becoming available – there's a beautiful red variety that cooks to a lovely soft shade of pink or there are mixed colours that will brighten up any meal.

GRAINS & PULSES

Peru cultivates a variety of indigenous and imported grains and pulses. Andean beans are grown alongside lentils and chickpeas. Quinoa is one of Peru's most famous exports, but other grains such as *kiwicha* (aramanth) and *kañiwa* are now finding their way into Europe.

BEANS
Beans are a staple to Peruvians as they grow extremely well, and because of the high levels of protein in them, they were often a good option when meat was scarce. Most commonly eaten are pinto, black butter beans (or Lima beans) and broad beans (called fava beans once boiled). At Ceviche we prefer to use fresh broad beans if they are in season, but they are becoming easier to find dried these days.

QUINOA
A few years ago quinoa was relatively unheard of. Fast forward a few years and quinoa is now beloved by healthfood aficionados. It is often wrongly described as a grain – it isn't, strictly speaking, as it doesn't come from the grass family. It is a seed, indigenous to the Peruvian Andes, that has long been valued for its nutritional content (it has high levels of protein, vitamins and minerals) and its nutty flavour.

RICE & WHEAT
Grains such as rice and wheat were brought to Peru by the Spanish and rice in particular has remained popular. It is generally served as a side dish, in soups and stews and in desserts. The Spanish had a huge influence on popularising the cultivation of wheat in Peru. Often used in baking, wheat berry is also very common, but you can use pearled barley or spelt instead.

MAIZE

Maize plays a huge part in the average Peruvian diet and is eaten in any number of ways. Because of the abundance of these crops they can be found in both savoury and sweet dishes. The two varieties most used are very distinctive in taste and appearance.

CHOCLO

Choclo is a large white variety of maize. The kernels have a creamy texture and the flavour is less sweet than the sweetcorn available in the UK. It can be boiled and eaten on the cob or sliced and added to stews and soups, puréed and used in tamales (see pages 56 and 58) and corn cakes (see page 134), or air-dried and ground into flour or meal and used in puddings. If you can't find it, you can substitute regular sweetcorn in all of the savoury dishes.

MAÍZ MORADO

This dark-purple corn has an intense, fruity flavour and turns a rich blackcurrant colour when cooked. In Peru it is the main ingredient of a popular soft drink, Chicha Morada (see page 213), and used in desserts, mixed with other fruits, spices and pisco. It is difficult to replicate exactly its dark berry-like flavour, but if you have to you could use any dark-purple fruit in its place, such as blueberries or blackberries.

HERBS

Peruvian cooking uses a lot of fresh coriander, bay leaves and dried oregano. These herbs are common in local supermarkets. One herb that may be trickier than most to track down and used often in Peruvian cooking is *huacatay*, or Peruvian black mint. If you do have trouble finding it, you can use a mix of tarragon, basil, coriander and mint instead. In particular at Ceviche, we like using micro herbs, such as basil and coriander. These are grown to the size of mustard or cress and if you can't find them in your local supermarket or greengrocers, try growing them in exactly the same way as cress on a windowsill; you should find that they sprout within days.

SPICES

Cumin appears in several savoury dishes and many Peruvians will use ground cumin in their seasoning. Cinnamon, cloves and nutmeg are used in sweet and savoury dishes and vanilla flavours everything from ice cream to Peruvian Dulce de Leche (see page 241). Annatto is another spice commonly found in Peruvian cooking, which is a bright-red seed native to Latin America and the Caribbean. This is used mainly for colour as it imparts a deep red ochre, but it also has a faintly peppery, spicy flavour. At Ceviche, we use a mixture of whole and ground spices in our dishes, such as the Huachana Sausage (see page 238). For the strongest flavour we recommend grinding the seeds in small quantities as and when you need them.

PISCO

This is the national drink of Peru. It is a clear spirit, distilled from very specific varieties of grape, and is the base of all of our cocktails, whether they are classics such as the Pisco Sour (see page 201) or ones we have created specifically for Ceviche like Soho Pisco (see page 207). While it is often used in its pure state, it is also infused with all kinds of aromatics, from chillies to coffee (see pages 216–217). We like to add a dash of it to all kinds of sweet and savoury dishes.

FRUIT

There are hundreds of different kinds of fruit in Peru. Avocados (our preferred variety is Hass), tomatoes, squash and red peppers are generally used in savoury dishes and also pineapple, papaya, soursop, custard apple, all kinds of mango, bananas, passion fruit and melons. I've listed some of the common fruit and their uses.

CITRUS FRUIT

Limes, oranges (including Seville oranges) and clementines were brought over by the Spanish and are loved throughout Peru. They not only add a certain liveliness to ceviches, salads and drinks, they also help to fine tune and balance the flavours of a dish. At Ceviche, we try to use

Peruvian, Brazilian or Japanese limes whenever we can. To get the most juice from a lime, wash it and roll it, applying gentle pressure to loosen the juice. Try not to over squeeze the lime, as bits of membrane can make the juice bitter.

PHYSALIS

Native to Andean forests, physalis were a favourite of high-ranking Inca families who cultivated them as well as sun-drying them. They have also been grown under polytunnel covers in the UK since the 18th century. Because of its distinctive appearance, each berry wrapped with its own paper Chinese lantern, it is most commonly used as a garnish if found outside Peru. Slowly, physalis is now being recognised for its flavour, which is excellent for jams, sauces and juices in both savoury or sweet dishes.

CUSTARD APPLE (CHIRIMOYA)

Once you've tried one you'll understand why it is called 'custard' apple. Peel away the skin (that can be any colour from green to dark brown), remove the large black seeds and you will be left with a pale-coloured flesh that is creamy in texture with a sweet, fruity, aromatic flavour.

LÚCUMA

This fruit is native to the Andes and is valued not only for its nutritional value (it is particularly rich in B vitamins and betacarotene) but for its creamy texture and very sweet flavour, which is reminiscent of maple syrup. It is rarely available fresh in the UK, but you can get it either in powder form (mix with water to a paste) from healthfood shops or frozen in pulp (see page 246). Although it may be hard to track down, it is definitely worth it as it makes a stunning sweetener in ice cream, creamy desserts or breakfast porridge.

PERUVIAN CHILLIES

The keystone of Peruvian cuisine is the chillies. There are numerous different varieties, but the bulk of what we use in the Ceviche kitchen is listed below. You can buy a huge variety of chillies and chilli pastes in food shops and online (see page 246). Many chillies can easily be substituted with others without the flavour of the overall dish being totally compromised so we've given some alternatives.

AMARILLO (AJÍ AMARILLO)

A very fruity and aromatic chilli with a gentle pepper flavour. It is similar to a scotch bonnet, but milder. Although a far cry from the real thing, its flavour can be imitated with a mixture of orange scotch bonnets tempered with some sweet orange or red pepper. A squeeze of orange juice wouldn't go amiss either. The dried version of this chilli is mirasol (*ají mirasol*), which shouldn't be confused with a fresh Mexican chilli of the same name.

LIMO (AJÍ LIMO)

This is a hot, spicy chilli, which, as its name suggests, has a very citrusy flavour, though we think it has more lemon in it than lime. Again, try a yellow scotch bonnet and perhaps squeeze some lemon juice over it if you're using it fresh rather than in a paste.

PANCA (AJÍ PANCA)

Panca is usually used as a dried chilli and imparts a smoky flavour and slight heat. It is often paired with other chillies to get a bit more heat. You can substitute these chillies with a combination of dried Kashmiri chillies and some hot smoked paprika. At a pinch, use chipotle, although this has quite a distinctive flavour all of its own.

ROCOTO

Don't be fooled by the larger size of this pepper. It looks benign, but really it's the exception to the rule that the larger the fruit, the milder the heat, as it scores highly on the Scotia scale. To substitute these peppers, use half a hot red chilli, preferably *habañeros*, and half a red pepper or tomato (generally, as a guide, one rocoto is about the same weight as half a red pepper).

CHILLI PASTES

Many of the recipes in this book will require chilli pastes. It is a good idea to make them in larger quantities than you will need for each recipe (you can store them in the freezer in an airtight container where the paste will stay fresh for 6 months). If you haven't the time or inclination to make the paste, you can instead blend some chilli with a little oil or water in a food processor or blender.

Using chillies in paste form is very convenient and versatile – they can be used in all kinds of dishes. They are absolutely indispensable to Peruvian cooking and therefore a mainstay in the Ceviche kitchen. We use them in mayonnaises as well as in vinaigrettes, sauces and soups.

BASIC CHILLI PASTE

This basic chilli paste works with any of the chillies on page 225, but the ones you'll find used most of all in this book are made with amarillo, panca or rocoto.

Put 1 tablespoon of vegetable oil in a large, heavy-based saucepan. Heat over medium heat and then add 100g frozen or fresh deseeded chillies of your choice or 35g reconstituted deseeded and roughly chopped dried chillies, and ½ a finely chopped small onion. Sauté over low heat for about 10 minutes, stirring regularly.

Add 2 crushed garlic cloves and sauté for 5 minutes until everything is very soft, being careful to make sure it doesn't take on any colour.

Put the contents of the saucepan into a food processor or blender and blitz until smooth. Store in the fridge in a sterilised jar (see Notes).

Makes about 190g.

NOTES

♦ If you are using dried chillies (such as panca chillies), dry roast them in a frying pan for 1–2 minutes and then cover with warm water to rehydrate. It may take several hours but the chillies should plump up almost to the point that they look fresh/frozen. Strain and deseed and you should end up with around 100g of chilli.

♦ If you are using rocoto, substitute half the quantity with sweet red pepper. This is because rocotos are very hot and the flavour needs balancing out a little.

♦ To sterilise glass bottles or jars, wash them in hot soapy water and place in a low oven (150°C/gas mark 2) until ready to use.

♦ As a general rule you can store chilli pastes for up to a week in the fridge. They will keep quite well if you decant into sterilised jars and cover with a layer of vegetable oil. And as mentioned earlier you can freeze them. A useful for tip for freezing is to put the paste into ice cube trays in tablespoon and teaspoon measurements and then decant into plastic bags once frozen.

LECHE DE TIGRE

TIGER'S MILK *This is a marinade of citrus juice (usually lime, but we also use Seville orange and clementine juices), salt and chilli used in our ceviche and* tiradito *recipes. Sometimes, garlic, ginger and coriander are added too. The marinade is made either by blending the ingredients and then straining it to give a smooth, slightly thicker sauce, or by infusing additional aromatics in the citrus juices so that it will be more liquid in consistency, with a subtler flavour.*

Every Peruvian will tell you that tiger's milk has miraculous properties; it's reputedly a stimulant and an aphrodisiac, and some say it cures hangovers. In Peru, once ceviche has been eaten, tiger's milk is never thrown out. In fact, it's often the case that more than needed is made up to be served as drinks (pictured left in glasses).

The following basic recipes make 120–150ml (enough to make a ceviche serving 4 people, made with about 600g fish).

TIGER'S MILK & PANTHER'S MILK

One of the best things about tiger's milk is that any leftover marinade can be used for making an array of refreshing drinks. Typically, once fish or seafood for a ceviche is ready to serve, some of the marinating liquid is strained off and can be served as a drink, imparting a hint of the sea.

You can use your tiger's milk as is, or blend it with other ingredients to stunning effect. Experiment with ingredients such as coriander leaves, squid ink or fruit to find a flavour you like. By adding a drop of pisco you will transform your tiger's milk into what we call panther's milk. Make a selection of ceviches and serve trios of tiger's or panther's milk in glasses alongside them to really appreciate the subtleties in flavour. You could also add a selection of the ingredients to decorate the glass, such as cucumber, celery, seafood and lime. A selection of tiger's or panther's milks served in shot glasses will also look great lined up in a row!

AMARILLO CHILLI TIGER'S MILK

This is our classic tiger's milk. It is probably the most versatile and the one we use most often at Ceviche.

Put a 5mm piece of fresh root ginger (cut in half), 1 small garlic clove (cut in half), 4 roughly chopped coriander sprigs and the juice of 8 limes in a bowl. Stir and then leave to infuse for 5 minutes. Strain the mixture through a sieve into another bowl. Add ½ teaspoon salt and 2 teaspoons Amarillo Chilli Paste (see page 226) and mix well. This will keep for 4 hours in the fridge.

NIKKEI TIGER'S MILK

This tiger's milk works best with any Nikkei-style ceviches or tiraditos.

Put a 5mm piece of fresh root ginger (cut in half), 1 small garlic clove (cut in half) and the juice of 8 limes in a bowl. Stir and then leave to infuse for 5 minutes. Strain the mixture through a sieve into another bowl. Add 2 teaspoons mirin, 2 teaspoons freshly squeezed orange juice, ½ teaspoon sesame oil and 1 tablespoon soy sauce and mix well. This will keep for 4 hours in the fridge.

ROCOTO TIGER'S MILK

This tiger's milk is much spicier than the rest, thanks to the rocoto, so it works best with strongly flavoured fish and seafood.

Put a 5mm piece of fresh root ginger, 1 small garlic clove, 50g deboned fresh white fish cuttings, 4 roughly chopped coriander sprigs and the juice of 8 limes in a bowl. Stir and then leave to infuse for 5 minutes. Transfer to a food processor or blender and blitz until smooth. Strain the mixture through a sieve into another bowl. Add ½ teaspoon salt and 2 teaspoons Rocoto Paste (see page 226) and mix well. This will keep for 2 hours in the fridge.

SAUCES, JAMS & OILS

AMARILLO CHILLI SAUCE

One of the best accompaniments, this chilli sauce will add a lovely fruity depth to any meat or fish dish.

Combine 50g Amarillo Chilli Paste (see page 226), 50g mayonnaise, 2 teaspoons red wine vinegar, 2 teaspoons vegetable oil, 2 crushed garlic cloves, a pinch of dried oregano and a pinch of salt in a bowl until well mixed and then set aside until needed. Ensure the texture is thick and not too watery. Makes about 100ml.

NOTE

♦ You can replace the Amarillo Chilli Paste with a blended mix of ½ a deseeded yellow pepper and ½ a deseeded yellow scotch bonnet.

HUANCAINA SAUCE

This is one of Peru's great sauces. At Ceviche we serve it as a dip alongside fried cassava or stirred through the Macaroni with Huancaina and Cheese Sauce (see page 116).

Heat a dash of olive oil in a frying pan over medium and sauté 1 chopped small white onion and 1 garlic clove until translucent. Transfer to a food processor or blender, add 4 tablespoons Amarillo Chilli Paste (see page 226), 100ml vegetable oil, 50g Fresh Cheese (see page 239) or feta and 350ml evaporated milk and blitz until smooth. Add 50g crushed cream crackers and blitz again. Add more oil, salt, crackers or even a squeeze of lime if needed to ensure you have the right balance of flavours and creaminess. Makes about 500ml.

ROCOTO JAM

This sweet chilli sauce uses Peru's finest, punchiest hot pepper and is perfect with seafood and meats or as an accompaniment to grilled vegetable dishes.

Put 5 deseeded and chopped red peppers, 2 deseeded and deveined rocotos and 4 crushed garlic cloves in a food processor or blender and blitz to a purée. If this looks too thick, add 200g peeled and chopped tomatoes as well – the liquid should help the process along. Put this purée into a large saucepan or preserving pan. Add 500g granulated sugar, 150ml red wine or cider vinegar and the juice of 2 limes.

Gently heat the mixture, stirring constantly until the sugar has dissolved. Turn up the heat, bring to the boil and then simmer, stirring regularly, until the mixture is well reduced and has a rich, sticky texture. Make sure you can see a clear expanse of the saucepan base when you drag a wooden spoon through the mixture. Remove from the heat and leave to settle, before skimming as necessary. Decant into sterilised jars (see page 227). This will keep well, sealed, but put in the fridge once opened. Makes about 1kg (or enough to fill 2 x 450g jars).

OLIVE SAUCE

This rich sauce keeps very well in the fridge and can be used for the Octopus in Olive Sauce (see page 77) and Coriander Potato Cake (see page 146) or as a dipping sauce.

Put 1 egg and 2 tablespoons lime juice in a food processor or blender and blitz together. Mix 200ml vegetable oil and 100ml extra virgin olive oil in a jug and gradually add it to the food processor with the motor running – once the mayonnaise has started to thicken and has emulsified, you can increase the speed. Add the 15 pitted Peruvian botija olives (or kalamata or any black olive) and blend until smooth. Add a dash of Worcestershire sauce and more seasoning if necessary. Store in the fridge for up to 1 week. Makes about 400ml.

NOTE
♦ Please don't be tempted to make the sauce purely with olive oil as it will taste far too strong.

UCHUCUTA SAUCE

This vibrant sauce is great as a dip or as an accompaniment to any meat and fish dishes.

Simply put 150g crumbled Fresh Cheese (see page 239) or feta, 2 tablespoons single cream, 1 tablespoon olive oil, 1 tablespoon Amarillo Chilli Paste (see page 226), 10g *huacatay* or a mixture of coriander, flat-leaf parsley, mint and tarragon and 50g Shallow-fried Corn (see page 53) in a food processor or blender and blitz until smooth. You could add more cream if needed to achieve a smooth consistency. Taste for seasoning and add salt if necessary. Makes about 200ml.

CORIANDER OIL

We use this a lot in the Ceviche kitchen. If you love coriander, it's worth making a large batch as it will keep in the fridge for around a month.

Put 1 small bunch of fresh coriander (leaves and stalks) in a saucepan with 100ml vegetable oil and set over medium heat. Heat gently for 5 minutes, without boiling, to let the coriander wilt. Take off the heat and leave it to cool. Transfer the coriander and oil to a food processor or blender and blitz until smooth. Strain through a fine sieve and decant into a sterilised bottle (see page 227). Store in a cool, dark place. Makes about 100ml.

SALSA

SALSA CRIOLLA

This basic salsa is more of a garnish than anything else. At Ceviche we alternate chopping techniques for the salsa to create different styles and textures but the ingredients always remain the same.

For a julienned salsa, finely slice 1 red onion, 2 cored and deseeded medium tomatoes and 2 deseeded and deveined rocotos as finely as you can. Soak the red onion in iced water for 10 minutes. Drain thoroughly and then mix with 1 tablespoon lime juice, 1 tablespoon olive oil and 2 finely chopped coriander sprigs. Season with salt and black pepper.

STOCKS

CHICKEN OR TURKEY STOCK

Various stocks are used in Peru to make the best broths and soups. Add some pasta, rice or pulses to this basic stock and you will have a fantastic dish.

Heat 1 tablespoon olive oil in a large saucepan over medium heat. Add 3–4 chicken carcasses or 1 turkey carcass and sauté for a few minutes until they start to take on some colour. Add 2 diced celery sticks, 1 diced onion, 2 diced carrots and 1 diced leek along with 2 bay leaves, 1 garlic clove and 1 teaspoon black peppercorns. Cover with 1.5 litres water, bring to the boil and remove any scum that collects on the surface. When this turns to a white foam, turn down the heat, simmer gently for 45 minutes and then strain. Pick over the carcasses and reserve any meat. Makes about 1.5 litres.

VEGETABLE STOCK

A lovely, simple vegetable stock that can be used in a variety of dishes.

Put 2 chopped celery sticks, 2 chopped onions, 2 chopped leeks, 3 chopped carrots, 4 fresh flat-leaf parsley sprigs, 1 fresh oregano sprig, 3 bay leaves, 1 teaspoon black peppercorns and 1 teaspoon allspice berries in a large saucepan and cover with 1.5 litres water. Simmer over low heat for 40 minutes. Strain and reserve the liquid, discarding everything else. Makes about 1.5 litres.

FISH STOCK

This recipe provides an excellent base for any fish soup, stew or sauce.

Put 200g of washed fish trimmings, 1 diced leek, 1 diced white onion, 1 diced celery stick, ½ a diced fennel bulb, 50ml white wine, 1 garlic clove, 1 teaspoon black peppercorns, 1 thyme sprig, 2 bay leaves and 1 litre cold water in a large saucepan or stockpot and cover. Simmer over medium heat for 5 minutes and then reduce the heat to very low and continue to simmer for 30 minutes. Strain and reserve the liquid. Makes about 1 litre.

VARIATION
♦ *Shellfish Stock* – sauté the heads and shells of prawns in olive oil and proceed as above. For added flavour use fish stock instead of water or add fish trimmings.

SAVOURY EXTRAS

SALCHICHA DE HUACHO

HUACHANA SAUSAGES *Making sausages is not something you're likely to do every day, but it is surprisngly easy if you have a sausage maker, which are available at a reasonable price online. Huachana sausages may look similar to a cooking chorizo, but the flavour is unique. You can order natural or artificial sausage casings online, but you will probably find that a friendly butcher will give you the length you need.*

Put 30g lard in a saucepan and melt over low heat. Add 1 teaspoon annatto seeds (see page 223). Leave for a few minutes – you should see the lard gradually change colour from yellow to a deep ochre. Strain the lard, discarding the seeds.

Put 600g minced pork shoulder, 1 tablespoon salt, ½ tablespoon freshly ground black pepper, 1 tablespoon Panca Chilli Paste (see page 226), 30g crushed garlic, 1 tablespoon ground cumin, 50ml red wine and 1 tablespoon red wine vinegar or Seville orange juice into a large, non-reactive bowl (glass is ideal) and mix thoroughly, rubbing the pastes, garlic and spices into the meat. If you can bear to use your hands to do this, please do. Cover and leave in the fridge to marinate for at least a few hours and preferably overnight.

When you are ready to make the sausages, wash the sausage casings with plenty of cold water. Put the end on the nozzle of your sausage maker and feed the meat through. If you don't have a sausage maker, you can improvise with an icing bag. Take care that you don't overstuff the sausage casings and that air pockets are kept to a minimum as both can result in the sausages splitting when you come to cook them. Twist the sausages into links around 12cm long and knot them at the end.

If you are using artificial casings, leave the sausages in the fridge overnight. Use within 2–3 days, or freeze until you want to cook them. Makes about 600g.

QUESO FRESCO

FRESH CHEESE *Also called 'farmer's cheese', this is a creamy and firm mild-tasting cheese. It has a slight hint of citrus and it's a bit like feta but less salty. It keeps its shape well when used in cooking and while it does soften, it won't melt. We use it interchangeably with feta, but it's very quick to make so well worth trying.*

Put 2.5 litres full-fat milk (raw if you can get it) in a saucepan with 1 tablespoon salt. Bring to the boil and immediately turn down the heat as low as possible. Add 3 tablespoons cider vinegar or lemon juice and start stirring – the milk will start separating into curds and whey. Keep stirring and if it looks as though it needs a bit more help to separate, add another tablespoon of vinegar or lemon juice.

Line a sieve or colander with a double layer of muslin or cheesecloth and place over a bowl. Strain the separated milk through the muslin and leave to stand for around 10 minutes. Bring the sides of the cloth together and squeeze very gently. The curds should have formed a solid mass of cheese.

The cheese is ready to eat from this point onwards. If you would like a firmer, drier texture, you can wrap it up in the cloth and sit it in the fridge with a weight of some sort over it for around an hour. The cheese will be fine in the fridge for 10–15 days. Makes 250–300g.

CHUÑO

ANDEAN DEHYDRATED POTATOES *For thousands of years potatoes have been a staple as they grow particularly well in Peru. They are often dried to lock in their flavour. Here is a simple method to make* chuño *at home.*

Preheat the oven to 200°C (gas mark 6).

Bake whole unpeeled potatoes in the preheated oven for 30 minutes. Don't cook them completely through. Transfer to the fridge for several hours until well chilled and firm.

It is up to you whether you peel the potatoes or not, but either way, do cut them into 2.5mm slices.

Either put in a dehydrator for around 12 hours or preheat your oven to its lowest setting (around 110°C/gas mark ¼) and spread the potato slices out evenly on a baking tray lined with baking parchment. Leave them in the oven, with the door ajar, for about 1 hour, then check them and turn every 30 minutes or so for the next few hours until the potato slices are brittle and pale in colour. Don't let them go orange or brown.

When completely dry and cool, store in a jar or plastic bag until needed; they should keep for 3–6 months in a cool, dry place (not the fridge).

TRADITIONAL METHODS

For a more traditional way of making *chuño*: freeze some whole unpeeled potatoes for 48 hours. Remove and defrost outside under the sun for 24 hours. Then place back in the freezer for another 48 hours. Take them out and as they defrost start to peel the skins off with your nails. Once peeled, squeeze gently and then harder to release as much water as possible. Leave these in a safe place, outside, facing the sky and away from animals or insects. The potatoes will turn black and go hard. Once they are dry and black, bring them inside and store.

SWEET THINGS

MANJAR BLANCO

PERUVIAN DULCE DE LECHE *This is the traditional recipe for* manjar blanco.

Put 200ml evaporated milk or single cream and 200ml condensed milk into a saucepan. Add a 3cm cinnamon stick, 3 cloves and 1 teaspoon vanilla extract (or 1 vanilla pod, split down the middle) and bring to the boil. When it has reached a rolling boil, turn down the heat and cook this mixture over low heat, stirring constantly to prevent it sticking to the bottom of the pan. When it has thickened (you will be able to draw a clear line through it with a wooden spoon) and turned a light caramel colour, remove from the heat. Strain and store in the fridge for up to a week. Makes about 380ml.

VARIATION

♦ For a quick version, open a can of condensed milk and stir in 1 teaspoon each of vanilla extract and cinnamon and a pinch of cloves. Sit the can in a saucepan three-quarter filled with water and leave to simmer very gently for 3–4 hours.

SUGAR SYRUP

You can buy this syrup, but it's much cheaper and quicker to make at home. It will keep for a couple of weeks in the fridge, but it is better fresh and chilled.

Measure 100g granulated sugar into a jug and pour over 100ml freshly boiled water. Stir until all the sugar has dissolved and then chill. A quick way to do this is to plunge the jug into a bowl of iced water. Alternatively, you can transfer to the fridge and leave until cold. Makes about 200ml.

HONEY SYRUP

A honeyed version of the above syrup. As honey has such a strong flavour, this recipe calls for quite different proportions to the sugar syrup (1:4 instead of 1:1).

Measure 25g honey into a jug and pour over 100ml freshly boiled water. Stir until all the honey has dissolved and then chill. A quick way to do this is to plunge the jug into a bowl of iced water. Makes about 125ml.

ELDERBERRY JELLY

This jelly is very useful in all kinds of savoury and sweet dishes. We also like to make it spiced with cinnamon or flavoured with orange zest and juice.

Put 1kg ripe elderberries, washed and stalks removed, in a saucepan and add enough water to almost, but not quite, cover them. Bring to the boil and then simmer for 15–20 minutes or until the berries are completely soft and the water is a dark reddish purple. Leave the liquid to strain through a jelly bag; this will take a few hours and you shouldn't rush it.

Measure the elderberry liquid into a measuring jug and note down how much liquid you have before pouring it into a large saucepan. For every 600ml, add 450g preserving sugar. Add the juice of 1 lemon and 1 lime and gently heat, stirring, for about 15 minutes or until the sugar has dissolved. Turn up the heat and allow to boil fiercely until setting point is reached. Test for setting by using a sugar thermometer, the temperature should be between 103–105°C. Remove from the heat and leave to settle. Skim off any scum that has surfaced and ladle into sterilised jars (see page 227). The jelly will keep for about a month if stored in the fridge. Makes about 1kg (or enough to fill 2 x 450g jars).

ELDERFLOWER LIQUEUR

Elderflower liqueur is fairly easy to get hold of, but is just as easy to make.

Simply stuff a large kilner jar with freshly picked elderflower heads and the zest of 1 lemon or lime, top up with vodka and leave to steep for up to a month. Strain the liquid, pour into a bottle (the old vodka bottle will do) and add 50–100g sugar depending on how sweet you like it. The liqueur is ready to drink as soon as all the sugar has dissolved. Makes about 1 litre.

PHYSALIS COULIS

This fruity coulis will add a sweet and jammy hit to any dessert.

Put 100g physalis (husks removed) in a saucepan with 50ml water. Add 50g caster sugar and simmer for about 15 minutes or until it has reduced and looks sticky and syrupy. Keep an eye on it as you don't want it to caramelise or burn. Add the juice of ½ a lime and then either blitz in a food processor or blender or strain through a sieve, ending up with a thick, jammy sauce. The coulis will keep for about a month if stored in the fridge. Makes about 150g.

SUPPLIERS

From Peruvian chillies, maize and choclo to pisco, the following websites should help you to find the specialist ingredients that appear in this book. Ceviche's online shop at www.cevicheuk.com/shop also stocks a variety of specialist Peruvian ingredients. We are continually growing our list of suppliers and own-produced or sourced products so check our website regularly for new updates.

CHILLIES
♦ **The Spice Shop**
www.thespiceshop.co.uk
♦ **Amigo foods**
www.amigofoods.com
♦ **South Devon Chilli Farm**
www.southdevonchillifarm.co.uk

MAIZE & CHOCLO
♦ **Mex Grocer**
www.mexgrocer.co.uk
♦ **La Bodeguita**
www.labodeguita.co.uk

MISCELLANEOUS
LÚCUMA POWDER
♦ **Indigo Herbs**
www.indigo-herbs.co.uk
MACA POWDER
♦ **Greens Organic**
www.greensorganic.co.uk
♦ **Buy Wholefoods Online**
www.buywholefoodsonline.co.uk
CORN HUSKS
♦ **Cool Chile**
www.coolchile.co.uk
ALFAJORES
♦ **Amisqi**
www.amisqi.com

BANANA LEAVES
♦ **Fine Food Specialists**
www.finefoodspecialist.co.uk
NORI SHEETS
♦ **Sushi Sushi**
www.sushisushi.co.uk
CASSAVA
♦ **Longdan**
www.longdan.co.uk
SOURSOP (GUANÁBANA) JUICE
♦ **Juna Fruits**
www.junafruits.com

PISCO & OTHER DRINKS
♦ **Amathus Drinks**
www.amathusdrinks.com
♦ **Gerrys Wines & Spirits**
www.gerrys.uk.com
♦ **The Whisky Exchange**
www.thewhiskyexchange.com
♦ **The Drink Shop**
www.thedrinkshop.com
BEER
♦ **Cusqueña**
www.cusquena.co.uk

ANTICUCHOS
CAUSAS
PISCO BAR
AMISTAD

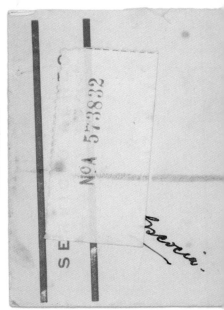

Lima: "Pila de la Plaza de Armas." (Perú)

10 ♦

CERTIFICADA

Cevichero te queremos

INDEX

IF YOU WOULD LIKE to visit us check out www.cevicheuk.com. I would love to hear from you with feedback on the food and techniques in this book. If you have any comments or an update on Peruvian suppliers to share, or a query about the recipes, please write to me at www.martinmorales.com or @martinceviche on Twitter.

ACKNOWLEDGEMENTS

We do this because we love it. At Ceviche we are true believers in our mission to present Peruvian food to all. Everyone I work with at Ceviche has passion and a great attitude and I have been very lucky to work with these exceptional people along the way.

Thank you very much to Amanda Harris, my publisher, for being a true believer from day one. I am indebted to Gregor Funcke for being my partner in writing this book and for checking and providing some of the recipes. Also, Alejandra Breustedt, a truly talented chef, as well as the brilliant Tom Halford, Miguel Arbe and Pamela Alderson who has worked with me since Ceviche was a mere idea.

Raquel de Oliveira is one of the most exceptional people I have ever had the pleasure of working with. You are key to our team and with so much passion and focus you lead by example, which is something I truly appreciate. Thank you to Clare Hulton for guiding me so brilliantly and enabling this book to happen. To Catherine Phipps for your thoughtful writing, dedicated editing and work on recipes. Your work has been invaluable to the completion of this book and you are a delight to work with. To our brilliant editor Abi Waters for working on every single word in this book and having the patience of a saint. To Camille Blais, Caz Hildebrand and Mark Paton at Here Design for understanding what we are trying to achieve as pioneers breaking new ground in this unique cuisine. To Paul Winch-Furness for capturing the essence of Ceviche in his photography right from the outset – it's great to work with someone who is truly passionate about food and has a unique, outstanding talent. Many thanks to Maria Fe Romero, Santiago Barco Luna, Solange Adum and Leslie Searles for some great photography based in Peru. Thanks to Annie Nichols for working so hard at our photoshoot cooking and styling alongside Polly Webb-Wilson in props. Thank you Diana Henry for providing us with a beautiful and comfortable set to work in.

Thank you to Lucie Stericker, Kate Wanwimolruk, Mark Rusher, Julia Pidduck and Elizabeth Allen for your dedication and incredible work in creating and launching this book. Thanks to Hannah Norris for being an exceptional publicist when launching Ceviche and to Richard Dawes at Dawbell for now helping us spread the message about our wonderful food. To Jack Schneider for designing a beautiful restaurant. To Devon Daley, Marc Connor, Nick Davis and Andy Guy, friends forever who supported me through thick and thin, especially thin. To the fantastic Cecilia Gorenflos for being Ceviche's number one supporter and helping us develop our work through all our activities. To all my family, especially June and Pat and Felix and Otilia Allen for making every day exciting and worth living for. And to Lucy, my wife and best friend, who has had to put up with my endless hours of work and supported me always with pure love.

Thank you to Sarah Bradley and Jenny Powles at Journey Latin America, Cusqueña, The Upper Scale and SSP for all your support in our projects.

So many more people have been involved in making this book and in our work at Ceviche, but special thanks go to Cam Chiappe, Alejandro Bello, Julian Bayuni, Ashlea O'Neill, David Buxton, Philippe Hails-Smith, Hayley Cross, Natalie Halsey, Ashley Herbert, Elsa Morales, Andres Morales, Daniel Morales, James Marshall, Duncan Ballantyne, Kitty Clark, Jim Beach, Stephen Quest, Alex Chesterman, Alvaro Benalcazar, Steffi Dellner, Photos Photiou, Erika Schuler, Jake Milligan, Mariano Alarco, Mylene Kaiser, Lindsay Faller, Nicole Goldstein, Ron Dann, Adrian Dann, Chariton Georgiou, Edward Filder, Graham Filmer, Kathleen Filmer, Oliver Schusser, Philippa Gill, Felipe Malpartida, Michael Acton Smith, Jack Schneider, Edith Shneider, Ol Beach, Ximena Guerrero, Alcira Sanchez, Nicole Merino, Lilian Amadi, Alejandro Chaparro, Effren Hermida, Helen Mulsow, Rossana Consiglieri, Laszlo Papp, Ana Perez Otero, Nicolas Saro Tejedor, Sabrina Leonardo, Cristian Tola Guerrero, Felix Schafer, Afzal Kaba, Philippa Gill, Felipe Malpartida, Helen Clarke, Juan Alonso Pastor, Adriano Rodriguez Somoza, Sergio Vargas Barreto, Juan Castro Espinoza, Luis Palacios Martinez, Kate Jameson, Luiz Bomfim De Sousa, Daniela Zago, Mitchell Cunningham, Virgilio Oliveira, Daniel Pacheco, Annette Langlois, Francesco De Sanctis and Alejandra Araujo Alvarez.

To Carmela, Oti and Dad. Wish you were here.

First published in Great Britain in 2013
by Weidenfeld & Nicolson
10 9 8 7 6 5 4 3 2 1

Text © Martin Morales 2013
Design and layout © Weidenfeld & Nicolson 2013

Food styling by Annie Nichols
Props styling by Polly Webb-Wilson
Edited by Abi Waters
Design, layout and art direction by Here Design

Photographs © Paul Winch-Furness
with the exception of
Pages 14–15, 60–61, 223 © Santiago Barco Luna
Pages 36–37, 84–85 © Leslie Searles
Pages 54–55, 101, 115, 122–123, 132–133, 180–181, inside front cover © Solange Adum
Pages 39, 63, 67, 87, 112–113, 138–139, 152–153, 162–163, 165, 244, inside back cover © Maria Fe Romero

A CIP catalogue record for this book is available from the British Library.

ISBN: 978-0-2978-6861-3

Printed and bound in China

Weidenfeld & Nicolson
The Orion Publishing Group Ltd
Orion House
5 Upper St Martin's Lane
London WC2H 9EA

An Hachette UK Company
www.orionbooks.co.uk

*Best efforts have been made to obtain permission for the use of artwork. If notified the publisher
will be pleased to rectify any errors or omissions at the earliest opportunity.*

*The Orion Publishing Group's policy is to use papers that are natural, renewable and recyclable
products and made from wood grown in sustainable forests. The logging and manufacturing
processes are expected to conform to the environmental regulations of the country of origin.*

Notes on the recipes

♦ Spoon measures are level and 1 tablespoon = 15 ml, 1 teaspoon = 5 ml.

♦ Preheat ovens before use and cook on the centre shelf wherever possible.
If using a fan oven, reduce the heat by 10–20°C.

♦ Medium free-range eggs have been used unless otherwise stated.

♦ All herbs are fresh unless otherwise stated.

♦ This book contains recipes made with raw eggs. Those with known allergic reactions
to eggs and egg derivatives, pregnant or breast-feeding women and very young children
should avoid recipes containing raw egg.

VISIT CEVICHE AT WWW.CEVICHEUK.COM